OTHER WORLDS

UFOS, ALIENS, AND THE AFTERLIFE

John R. Heapes, MA, MSW

iUniverse LLC
Bloomington

iUniverse books may be ordered through booksellers or by contacting:

iUniverse LLC
1663 Liberty Drive
Bloomington, IN 47403
www.iuniverse.com
1-800-Authors (1-800-288-4677)

Because of the dynamic nature of the Internet, any web addresses or links contained in this book may have changed since publication and may no longer be valid. The views expressed in this work are solely those of the author and do not necessarily reflect the views of the publisher, and the publisher hereby disclaims any responsibility for them.

Any people depicted in stock imagery provided by Thinkstock are models, and such images are being used for illustrative purposes only.
Certain stock imagery © Thinkstock.

ISBN: 978-1-4917-2190-2 (sc)
ISBN: 978-1-4917-2189-6 (hc)
ISBN: 978-1-4917-2188-9 (e)

Library of Congress Control Number: 2014901903

Printed in the United States of America.

iUniverse rev. date: 02/19/2014

To my grandchildren—Quinn, Eli, Cole, and Antonio—who are the joys of my life

CONTENTS

PREFACE

The idea behind this book arose from two areas. First, teaching college-level sociology for over forty-five years; second, in the 1970s and 1980s, I happened upon books written about unidentified flying objects (UFOs) and the near-death experience (NDE). The confluence of these two sources led me to wonder how societies might be structured in "other worlds."

In the mid-1970s, I read Raymond Moody's *Life After Life*, where he introduced the American audience to the NDE. Moody explained that his interest in the subject arose from a book he read by George Ritchie, *Return from Tomorrow*. In the 1980s, Dr. Ritchie came to dinner with my wife and me after speaking at Harrisburg Area Community College in Pennsylvania. His NDE story enthralled us, and the quality of the man captivated us as well; he was humble and sincere.

Around that time, I stumbled upon Raymond Fowler's *The Andreasson Affair* (1979). This book recounts the story of Betty Andreasson, who claimed she had been abducted by aliens. After reading Fowler's book, I read *The Interrupted Journey* (1966) by John Fuller. This was the first American book about alien abduction of humans. During the 1980s, more books on these topics appeared. Budd Hopkins (*Missing Time*, 1981), Whitley Strieber (*Communion*, 1987), and a host of other authors wrote about encounters with aliens from other planets. Both the NDE and UFO/abduction literature were describing worlds other than Earth. As a sociologist, I wondered whether these places had societies with institutions like governments and economies. Did they have values and norms (i.e., socially approved rules)? Did they stratify their people into social classes as earthlings do? Therein began the search that culminated in writing this book.

The purpose of this book is not to prove or disprove the existence of extraterrestrials (ETs) and/or life after death. The approach is much like the sociology of religion, which does not seek to prove or disprove God's existence; rather, this discipline describes the effect of the belief in God on the behavior of individuals. For instance, the sociologist of religion would ask, "Does a person's belief in God affect whom he or she votes for?"

A Google search of UFOs alone yielded 178 pages of references. Although there are thousands of books on this topic, and many written about the NDE as well, none of them describe the social structure of these other worlds. To date, no books in sociology cover this subject matter.

There are fields that study extraterrestrial life, such as xenology and astrobiology, which is a more commonly accepted reference for the study of ETs, according to this literature.[1] Likewise, although there is no NDE discipline, traditionally established areas of study, such as psychology and biology, examine this phenomenon. However, xenology, astrobiology, and NDE-related fields do not study the social structure of societies inhabited by aliens and the dead.

Please be cautious while reading this book; it has limitations. First, it should not be read as an affirmation of these phenomena. This book does not endeavor to establish or to discredit the reality of life after death and aliens living on other planets. Second, this is not a sociological study with hypotheses to be tested. Rather, the book falls into the scope of an exploratory study that precedes the development of hypotheses. After reading this book, one might hypothesize that more men than women see UFOs, or that more women than men have NDEs. A researcher may then draw a sample from a topic area and test the validity of the assertion.

Much is written about UFOs and NDEs. There are scores of questions in the UFO literature. For instance, are there UFOs and aliens? Is the government covering up UFOs? Are ETs landing on Earth? Likewise, in the NDE arena, there are many controversial topics. Is there life after death? Does consciousness extend beyond death? Are these near-death experiencers (NDErs) dead?

All of these questions, although intriguing and critical, are not covered in this book. The only question under scrutiny is: *How are the social worlds of aliens and those on the other side of life structured?* For instance, do beings in these worlds occupy statuses (e.g., student) and play roles (e.g., take exams)? Are their societies stratified into upper and lower social classes? Do they have institutions, such as marriage, government, and education? Do these places have social problems, such as unemployment, prostitution, and war?

As a sociologist, I am qualified to sociologically examine these other worlds. I taught college-level sociology courses for over forty years. Two popular courses were the Sociology of the Future and the Sociology of Other Worlds. I examined over 2,400 cases in the NDE and UFO areas. I also read numerous books and articles on both of these subjects. Finally, I spoke with scores of people who saw UFOs or had NDEs.

I invite you to now commence a long journey with me. Be prepared to go to distant places in other galaxies and to a different time: a time after all of your tomorrows. You will meet humans making incredible claims about realities beyond anything imaginable. As you take this trip, you may wonder if the social world of aliens and those in the afterlife are similar to societies on Earth. Are there universal laws governing the social structures of intelligent beings no matter where they reside in existence? Are humans projecting into foreign forms their own beliefs about how social structures should be arranged on Earth? An affirmative answer to the first question assumes that these distant places exist. An affirmative response to the second question presupposes that such distant places do not exist.

ACKNOWLEDGMENTS

My sincere thanks go to Harrisburg Area Community College (HACC—Central Pennsylvania's Community College) for its support of this project: Sheila Ciotti for permission, Diane Trullinger for technical assistance, and Professor David Liu for support and idea-sharing. Also, recognition goes to Dr. Gale Peter Largey, Professor Emeritus at Mansfield University, Pennsylvania, for his lifelong support of these intellectual pursuits.

Special recognition goes to my wife, Sheila, who kept me grounded as I researched these topics.

INTRODUCTION

How are the worlds of aliens from other planets and of people living on the other side of death socially arranged? Are these worlds organized in the same manner as they are on Earth? For example, do these social worlds have institutions, such as governments and the military?

This book examines the social makeup of other worlds. This study has three necessary components: (1) the meaning of other worlds; (2) the meaning of social worlds; and (3) the ways in which these other worlds are studied.

What Are "Other" Worlds?

Social sciences, such as psychology, sociology, anthropology, history, and economics, study the human aspects of life on Earth.[1] Anthropology is known in the United States as a discipline that studies societies other than its own. For instance, a US citizen picking up an anthropology book might expect to read a description of a tribe in the Amazon jungle of Brazil.

The word *other*, as used in this book, has a fundamentally different meaning than the one employed by anthropology. Anthropology studies earthly societies. The sociology of other worlds examines societies in worlds beyond Earth (that is, in the ecto realm).[2] Two types of ecto-level societies are observed in this book: the worlds of aliens and the world of those inhabiting the afterlife. We will examine the domains left by aliens when they came to Earth in their UFOs; we will also examine the world seen by people who had NDEs. Are these worlds similar to or different from the social worlds populated by humans on Earth? For example, do aliens and the deceased marry, divorce, and remarry as earthlings do? Do other worldly beings (OWBs) practice religion as earthlings do? Do OWBs organize their social worlds as earthlings do?

Why cover UFOs and NDEs in the same book? What is the connection between them? There are two ways of conceptualizing UFOs and NDEs. First, think in terms of material and nonmaterial. The UFO side presents us with concrete items, such as spacecraft and aliens, while the NDE side gives us nonmaterial elements, such as spirits and heaven. Second, consider a space/time continuum. The UFO phenomenon focuses on the sphere of space, while the NDE occurrence concentrates on the province of time. In other words, NDEs expose an "other world" somewhere after a human's last tomorrow. Together, UFOs and NDEs offer data about truly other worlds—ones that are different from the one we currently live in.

What Is Sociology? What Is the Sociological Perspective?

In this book, we will seek an understanding of how aliens and beings on the other side of life organize themselves into groups and societies. The outlook we use in pursuit of this understanding is the sociological perspective.

The social sciences include such disciplines as psychology, economics, and sociology. These social science disciplines present concepts to help us understand how social worlds work.[3] Therefore, examination of alien societies' operation, as well as scrutiny of the afterlife's social world, represents a sociological study.

How does a sociologist see a social world? Imagine a photographer taking a picture with a camera. She sets her 35 mm camera lens on a house and its surroundings. When she changes the camera's lens to 70 mm, the landscape crowds out as the house comes in and more detail reveals itself. What a photographer sees in each picture depends upon which lens (i.e., 35 mm or 70 mm) she uses.

Consider that the lenses described above are not glass but concepts. Just as different millimeter sizes reveal distinct objects so, too, do unlike concepts unveil different worlds. For instance, if a person employs such concepts as *galaxy*, *stars*, and *nebulae*, he or she will see the universe. This is the astronomical lens! If an individual looks through such concepts as *electron*, *proton*, and *atom*, he or she sees a much smaller world: the subatomic space. This is the physics lens!

Clearly, when looking through a lens or a concept, the viewer has a certain perspective on the world. If a person looks through concepts of zoology, he or she sees animals. If, however, this individual looks through psychological concepts, he or she perceives personalities. If an individual looks through sociological concepts, he or she draws society into focus. For instance, a sociologist may use *norms* to explain where on a road people should drive cars. In the United States, the rule is to drive on the right-hand side of the road, while in England, people drive on the left-hand side.

How Are These Other Worlds Studied?

The method used in the study of alien worlds and the afterlife is *content analysis*. In a book of sociological readings by Ksenych and Liu, the authors provide Robert Weber's definition of content analysis: "a research methodology that utilizes a set of procedures to make valid inferences from text."[4] Ksenych and Liu go on to say that "content analysis investigates a group's culture and social structure indirectly by studying the content of the communication and cultural artifacts of group members."[5] According to these authors, a researcher is studying a group indirectly when he or she is examining its communication and cultural artifacts.

I have neither gone to an alien society nor visited life after death. I have neither directly studied the communication and artifacts of aliens nor those who populate the other side of life. Rather, I have read books by people claiming a visit to another planet or contacting aliens. Also, I have read books by or about people who visit the afterlife and describe what they see. This book is a sociological description of what these people hear and/or see relative to beings living in these other worlds.

Summary

We must be cautious when drawing conclusions concerning these other worlds. Do these places exist? This question, although necessary, is not under scrutiny for our purposes. Rather, our interest lies in understanding how aliens and afterlife beings construct their social worlds. Their existence is a moot point. Second, because the books examined by me during the course of my research were written by different people, they may describe different worlds, not the same one(s). For instance, are gray and black men in the UFO literature from the same planet or different planets? The assumption made in this book is that they are from the same planet unless explicit documentation indicates otherwise.

Finally, why study such ethereal and controversial material? Is it not a waste of time, especially if these places do not exist? Perhaps, but we always learn about ourselves when we study those who are different from us, whether those beings are real or not. Anyone who has read a good book of fiction knows the validity of this point. Consider how many young people identify with Harry Potter and his friends in the *Harry Potter* book series, or, more recently, with the teens in the *Hunger Games* books.

What follows is a presentation of the sociological perspective. We will explore the origin of the social world of humans on Earth. With this sociological perspective in hand, we will be able to compare and contrast Earth's societies with alien and afterlife social worlds.

PART I
SOCIOLOGY

1

WHAT IS SOCIOLOGY?

Sociology Defined

According to David Dressler, sociology is "[T]he scientific study of human interaction. It is also the body of knowledge about human interaction resulting from such study."[1] Society, according to sociologists, is the largest group. It is millions of interactions among people occupying a common territory, such as a country.

The primary subject matter of sociology is human interaction. But what is *interaction*? A person sending a meaningful or understandable message and another responding in a like manner constitute interaction. A sociologist observes and identifies interaction, looking for patterns. He or she then examines how these patterned responses affect interaction among people.

There are verbal and nonverbal interactions. Thus, a sociologist might wonder if nice words spoken between people generate interaction different from (or the same as) harsh words exchanged. For instance, consider that one's persistent message to another person is, "You're such a great person. I admire everything about you." While the other's persistent response is, "Thank you. I think highly of you too." Now consider that one's persistent message to another person is, "You are the meanest, most vile person I've ever met." While the other's persistent response is, "You are the most uncaring, self-centered person that has ever existed." Do these nice and harsh words generate the same or different responses from these people in interaction?

3

Although interactions are most often verbal, they can be nonverbal. For instance, do facial expressions like frowns generate the same responses from others as smiles do? Similarly, does placing one's index finger and middle finger in a V shape receive the same response as raising only one's middle finger?

The following is a familiar but uncommonly studied aspect of human interaction. It is presented to illustrate how sociology might study a social phenomenon. Everyone smells! People give out odors, and they smell them. Focusing on the part where people give off odors, imagine one person is nine months old and the other is sixteen months old.[2] They are playing together in a playpen. They are smiling at one another as they play. Further imagine the nine-month-old lets go "a load" in his or her diaper. What happens between the two after "the event" as compared to before it? Probably nothing changes; they just keep playing together.

But what happens when the age of people in interaction changes? Does their behavior alter in the same situation? For example, if the two people playing together are nine *months* old and sixteen *years* old. Imagine what happens when the nine-month-old lets go "a load" in his or her diaper now. Does this action change the interaction going on between them? The answer is yes. The sixteen-year-old probably says, "Ugh! You stink!" And then the teenager takes the baby to change his or her diaper. They move from playing together to engaging in an act of hygiene.

Clearly, in the first case, age makes no difference in the interaction between people, but in the second situation it does.

Sociology studies the interaction going on among people in an effort to understand what it is and how it affects people's behavior toward one another. As variables like age, sex, race, and social class change, sociologists see if these variables affect how people act toward one another. For example, a sociologist might ask, "Does the age of a person affect how that individual tolerates TV violence?" This might lead to a more specific question, such as, "Do people under twenty-one years old tolerate it more than those over sixty-five?"

What Is the Sociological Perspective?

When we look at the world sociologically, we look at it through sociological concepts. These concepts function as a frame of reference, enabling holders of the perspective to see elements of the social world that are invisible to those without this perspective. Sociologists call this way of viewing the *sociological imagination,*[3] *sociological consciousness,*[4] or, more simply, the *sociological perspective.*

Peter Berger describes the sociological imagination as the ability to penetrate the "official level of meaning or reality" in order to see other levels, which he refers to as the "unofficial levels of meaning or reality."[5] Using sociology as a form of consciousness, a person can penetrate what most people, most of the time, understand about the social world. They can then see other levels of meaning and reality. For instance, if asked what the purpose of babysitting is, most parents say, "It is to provide adult supervision for children when the parents are not home." This explanation represents Berger's official level of meaning or reality. The sociological perspective allows one to see things differently.

Using such sociological concepts as, *exploitation, power,* and *minority group*, one understands babysitting in a new way. It becomes a social activity where powerful figures (i.e., parents) exploit the work of a minority group (i.e., young babysitters) by paying them low wages. Why? Because it enables parents to get away from their "little barbarians" in order to save their marriages. However, one never hears parents describe babysitting this way; they always explain it in the "official" manner.

Take note here: sociologists do *not* claim that people are lying when they describe the social world in the official way. The sociological imagination merely permits other ways of understanding the familiar. As such, it provides one with insight into those things usually taken for granted.

Thus, sociology is a social science discipline made up of concepts that enable viewers to see society. There are hundreds of sociological concepts, such as *culture, folkways,* and *deviance.* Their numbers are numbing. How does a novice grasp the sociological perspective with its myriad concepts? The following section offers a diagram that pulls significant sociological concepts together for easy application. The diagram (i.e., diagram-for-social-living) is in the form of a story. The story tells the origin of social living on Earth.

Adam and Eve in the Garden of Sociology: An Introduction to the Sociological Perspective

The Diagram-for-Social-Living[6]

Imagine you are a traveler in a machine that propels you back in time. You go back into the twentieth century, speeding back in time through the nineteenth and eighteenth centuries. You pass the Industrial Revolution and Columbus boarding the Santa Maria for the Americas. You accelerate the machine, racing through eons of time. You flash past the invention of farming. You sojourn back even further in time, through the age of hunters and gatherers. The time machine slows down and stops at its destination. You find yourself among the first humans, and you wonder about their origin. You ponder the possibilities. Did God or evolution create these first people?

Having no current interest in this compelling question, as a time-traveling sociologist, you concentrate on what is happening to humans after their arrival on Earth. You seek an understanding of how humans organize themselves to meet their needs.

In the beginning, these first humans, through trial and error, learned that penis inserted into vagina was pleasurable. Further, they realized that this pleasurable activity produced offspring, providing humanity with a future. For those who did not make this connection, their line became extinct.

Emphasizing the significance of this activity and managing the pragmatics of it, human groups created words to describe this species-saving action. For example, they tagged the anatomical parts (i.e., penis and vagina) and they named the involving action (i.e., intercourse). They created customs (i.e., marriage ceremonies) to highlight the significance of this event, and they developed rules

6

or norms to regulate the act of intercourse (e.g., it is a private act not to be done in public). These words, customs, and norms formed a framework for understanding, and this served as a strategy for engaging in intercourse.

Groups create this framework and pass it to future generations (via socialization) as answers to questions about reproduction. It becomes a *diagram-for-social-living*[7] as it relates to sexual relations. Each group creates its own diagram. What may be on one group's diagram-for-social-living may not be on another. For instance, in some groups, having many wives or husbands at the same time is appropriate; in other groups it is totally inappropriate.

More broadly, the diagram-for-social-living is a socially created blueprint guiding group members as they seek ways of dealing with *problems-in-living*. This diagram designates out of all possible behaviors those which are appropriate, right, and normal. For each problem-in-living, a group creates another diagram-for-social-living. With the passage of time, these diagrams become background assumptions for behavior. Group members accept them as taken-for-granted beliefs about how things are and should be. For instance, for many, sex with other humans is normal, while intercourse with a dog is not.

Moving from prehistoric to contemporary times, we notice that there are only a few situations in today's society where a social situation is not already defined. Most situations have preexisting diagrams governing how people act toward one another. Take a few moments. Try to think of social situations that have no preexisting rules of conduct. You may think of one or two, but these are likely to be rare events. A riot comes to mind.

It is difficult to become aware of diagrams imbedded in us. We simply take them for granted. For instance, we do not wonder what side of the road to drive on when entering a car. We automatically go to the right side (unless in a country where driving is on the left side).

To get a perspective on these diagrams, we can go back in time when humans first created them. In other words, we shall seek the sociological beginning.

Discovering the Sociological Beginning

In the sociological beginning, there were two people.[8] According to Western tradition, they were Adam and Eve. Both of them had needs, as individuals and together. They had physical and social needs.[9] These needs were either real or perceived.[10] As a result of their interaction, Adam and Eve found ways of satisfying their needs. Imagine the events outlined below.

Probably, the first human dilemma faced by Adam and Eve was how to initiate an exchange. That is, how to start a conversation between themselves. One may have smiled toward the other and said something. Surely, sometime later one of them invented a greeting like, "Hello!" or "How are you?" These words then became a mechanism for initiating an interaction. Eventually, the other responded, "Fine. How are you?" These expressions may be the first examples of social interaction.

Other problems-in-social-living were faced by Adam and Eve. For instance, after a few days of walking through the garden, undoubtedly they experienced pain[11] in their stomachs. Eve may have grabbed her stomach and grimaced; as did Adam. In amazement, they realized they were feeling the same pain, and one said to other, "I'm hungry." Indicating agreement, the other smiled. These expressions of hunger between them may be the second example of social interaction.

Adam and Eve walked into the garden in search of food. Out of all possible vegetative, animal, and fish life present, they learned through trial and error which of these life forms satisfied their hunger need. For example, if they ate little blue balls (i.e., blueberries) off bushes and these satisfied their hunger, they probably looked for blueberries the next and every subsequent time they experienced hunger pangs. Also, they repeated the way in which they collected these berries[12] because this method of picking them satisfied their hunger.

Thus, berry-picking methods, once established, are regularized. One action follows another in the same sequence each time they went berry-picking. Simply stated, there was a pattern, or structure, to their berry-picking activity.[13]

Elements of social structure include such notions as statuses, roles, norms, values, and groups. For instance, after several berry-picking trips into the garden, through their interaction with one another, Adam was established as the limb-bender, and Eve, the berry-picker (i.e., *statuses*). Adam and Eve picked out a bush, and Adam pushed it over while Eve picked the berries from it. The actions performed by Adam and Eve in their statuses are *roles*. At some point in time, Adam and Eve considered themselves as belonging together, and they became a *group*.

Adam and Eve probably got into a pattern of picking berries in the same way, and later they expected each other to behave in this manner. When one of them acted differently, probably the other scolded that person (i.e., gave a *negative sanction*). These expected ways of behaving became guidelines for the way limbs were to be bent, and berries picked. They became their *norms*. Norms are rules guiding people in their behavior. Moreover, since berries and the method by which to get them met their needs, this food and this approach became *valued*; that is, preferred.

Social structure, or the diagram-for-social-living, is visualized as shown in figure 1.1.

$$\underline{\quad\quad}|\underline{\quad\quad\quad\quad}|\underline{\quad\quad}$$

FIGURE 1.1: The Diagram-for-Social-Living.

This diagram organizes people's behavior in any situation or place where two or more people are together (i.e., *social situation*). Therefore, out of all possible behavior (represented by the horizontal line in the diagram) some behaviors (found inside the vertical lines on the diagram) are specified by groups as appropriate, right, and normal. Behaviors found outside the vertical lines are seen as inappropriate, wrong, and abnormal or *deviant*. Hence, members of a nudist colony have a diagram establishing "wearing *no* clothes in public" as appropriate. However, most people living in Pennsylvania have a diagram informing them that such behavior is not only inappropriate but also abnormal, wrong, and deviant. Diagrammatically, this example looks like figure 1.2.

Nudist Colony	**Pennsylvanians**
—| Do *not* wear clothes |—	—| *Do* wear clothes |—

FIGURE 1.2: Application of the Diagram-for-Social-
Living to a nudist colony and to Pennsylvanians.

The Socialization Process

How did Adam and Eve's offspring understand how to satisfy their
needs? How did they know how to behave correctly in a social
situation? In this presentation, how did they grasp their group's
diagram-for-social-living?

Pangs of hunger are natural or inborn, but the ways to satisfy them
are learned. For instance, some people eat hamburgers when they are
hungry, while others eat guinea pigs (in Peru).[14] Humans are not born
with knowledge of how to solve their problems-in-social-living. This
knowledge is acquired through association with other humans, by
means of a process called *socialization*.

A person (or a thing, such as a book or movie) teaching a diagram
through socialization is a *socializing agent*. A learner in this process is
a *socializee*. Therefore, Adam and Eve taught their sons what foods to
eat. Similarly, they taught Cain and Abel how to bend bushes over
to get the food that provided sustenance for them. However, if these
boys ate apples instead of blueberries, their parents considered them
deviant.[15] Cain and Abel knew their parents got angry when they ate
the wrong fruit, and they knew they would be punished (i.e., given a
negative sanction). Conversely, when the boys ate the right fruit, they
conformed to their parents' wishes. Cain and Abel knew their parents
would be happy with them, and they might get a reward, such as extra
blueberries for breakfast (i.e., receive a *positive sanction*).

Why did Adam and Eve exert so much energy to get Cain and
Abel to behave? One reason has to do with power.[16] Why were
Adam and Eve interested in exercising power over their children?
To understand what is gained by using power, one must examine the
results of socialization for the group (e.g., Adam and Eve's family) and
for the individual (i.e., Cain or Abel).

As previously stated, Adam and Eve had diagrams in their heads[17] guiding them as they solved problems-in-social-living. For example, diagrams informed them how to gather food for satisfying their hunger. Furthermore, if their children followed their diagram for food-gathering, all of them would be doing it in the same way; consequently, at minimum, they did not get in each other's way. Clearly, there was order in the group (i.e., *social order*). Also, when Adam and Eve were not present, they still got their children to act as they wished. How? The diagrams in their children's heads directed them to act in their parents' way. For instance, if Adam directed Cain to cooperate with his brother and Cain did not do it, probably Cain felt bad or guilty. Why? He deviated from Adam's norms.

Even in the absence of their parents, children still behave. Why? Their parents are in the children's heads in the form of diagrams-for-social-living. Furthermore, when members of a group, such as a family, act off the same diagram, there is order in that social unit. Thus, power is exercised over an individual, as well as a social situation, through content on diagrams. Simply, parents exerted power over their children's behavior when the children followed their parents' diagrams, which were in the children's heads.

Thus, through socialization, a socializee acquires diagrams-for-social-living to solve his or her problems-in-living. As an individual acts off these socially constructed diagrams-for-social-living, his or her behavior becomes predictable, and, consequently, group behavior becomes orderly.

Culture

The first humans solved problems-in-living when they repeated successful behaviors. As humanity's first family worked together to solve problems-in-living, they repeated behaviors that netted them their desired results. These roles were performed in statuses (e.g., limb-bender) occupied by the first family's members. They established norms that showed them how to behave. They valued these ways because they helped them to satisfy their needs. Together, statuses, roles, norms, and values formed a social structure (or diagram-for-social-living). This social structure was created from this family's interactions with each other. When they acted from this diagram, it ordered their behavior.

Actions in the berry-picking incident represent only one pattern of behavior. Living in the physical world, Adam and Eve needed to solve numerous problems-in-living. These included situations, such as creating words to identify objects in nature and building shelters to protect themselves against a sometimes harsh climate.

Culture is a people's design, diagram, or map for living. Maps help people across unfamiliar territory, while culture aids people in solving their problems-in-living. Culture contains material and nonmaterial items. These items help people survive and thrive. Some examples of the material aspects of culture are stones tied to sticks (used as hammers) and nuclear power plants (used for generating electrical power). Examples of the nonmaterial elements of culture are the custom of shaking a hand upon greeting or believing hard work will get a person ahead in life.

If society is the largest group, *how* that group lives is its culture. A society occupies a physical territory and participates in a common culture. Culture is a society's "game plan" or diagram-for-living.

Over time people become *enculturated*. They become immersed in their culture to a point where their diagrams-for-social-living seem natural to them. In other words, people take their culture for granted.

Culture is similar to a dip into which a group is immersed. Members come to understand themselves, others, and reality, depending upon the content of their dip. Suppose people are dipped into a culture where its technology is stones tied to sticks for hammers. They are asked to identify a typical object in a kitchen. They are likely to name a clay pot or a fire pit. If, however, others are dipped into a culture where its technology includes nuclear power plants, they are likely to describe a microwave oven in their kitchen. Neither respondent gives an answer of the other because their own culture does not permit them. Simply, humans are bound to their culture (i.e., *culture bound*). For example, Cain and Abel automatically went to blueberry bushes for food because their culture told them what to eat.

Culture gives people strategies for solving problems-in-living, and, usually, a person does not think twice about these solutions. For instance, in contemporary American culture people do not think about which piece of silverware they should use for eating peas. They automatically pick up a fork. Why? Culture gives them an answer. In other words, people internalize a diagram-for-social-living that tells them which silverware to use.

A person who follows the content on his or her group's diagram, and thereby successfully solves a problem, may come to believe his or her diagram is superior to another group's. For instance, when Adam and Eve came upon another group who ate apples, they may have believed the other group's solution inferior. They may have thought the apple tasted bad, compared to blueberries. Sociologically speaking, Adam and Eve were ethnocentric. *Ethnocentrism* is the belief one's diagram, culture, or way of life is superior to another's.

How does a group's solutions (or diagrams) to problems-in-living reach subsequent generations? Skills and knowledge are not inherited. Diagrams that organize behavior are passed on through language. Language is a set of symbols put together in an infinite number of ways for the purpose of communicating meaning.[18] Clearly, language is a medium through which a group's diagrams are transmitted (i.e., *cultural transmission*) to members who have not yet learned them (e.g., youngsters or immigrants).

Adam and Eve taught Cain and Abel which natural objects helped them to survive. They initially grunted and groaned, or smiled and nodded, to differentiate bad from good. A more efficient method of communicating, and one that Adam and Eve discovered, was language. It was first spoken and later written. Adam and/or Eve may have created the following symbols: *edible* associated with blueberry, and *inedible* was associated with apple. Similarly, edible and blueberries were considered "good," while inedible and apples were "bad."

Reality was defined for Cain and Abel when they understood the meanings attached to each symbol. When the boys ate blueberries, they simultaneously satisfied their hunger and defined their identity. They were "good" for eating their group's preferred food. Likewise, a contemporary American probably feels normal when eating a hamburger but weird consuming a dog. However, the people in the southern region of China find dogs a delectable delight![19]

Language defines reality and also serves as a medium through which culture is transmitted. The language a person is taught influences what aspects of the world he or she sees. For instance, the term *gentrification* allows an American to *see* urban decay turned into middle-class housing, but a Brazilian will not see this phenomenon in Rio de Janeiro until after learning this term.[20]

The Sapir-Whorf thesis advances the proposition that language shapes people's thinking and perception.[21] Reality is either constructed or influenced by language and culture. People determine/influence what they see in the world, depending upon which language and culture they learn. Humanity's first family saw blueberries and not apples as food.

Society Grows, Differentiates, and Stratifies: From Micro to Macro Levels of Social Living

Humanity constituted a small group when it contained only Adam's family. As such, it was a whole unit. Humanity's small group grew as this family expanded from two to four to a million and more. Society created mechanisms organizing people to satisfy their needs. Some of these mechanisms were groups, bureaucracies, cities, and nation-states. In other words, society differentiated into units that dealt with problems-in-living and that met needs for survival.

As society grows, tasks-for-living increase. One person can organize and direct four people to gather food, but doing the same task requires many more supervisors when there are a thousand workers, not four. Increasing the population size yields a concomitant increase in the number of functions (i.e., tasks, jobs) that a society will need to fill.

Group members shared what they had in the beginning because resources were scarce. Then humanity's technology developed and became more sophisticated. The mechanisms of social organization (e.g., communities), operating efficiently, generated a surplus of resources. Groups stratified when some accumulated more resources than others. Those with more desired objects (e.g., blueberries or money) held higher positions than those with fewer resources.[22] In other words, inequality emerged as societal members permitted some to accumulate more than others.

Institutions

Humanity grew in size from one family into larger social units, such as tribes. As it did, its tasks-in-living multiplied, and the entire pattern of social living became more complex. Rules directing four people are fewer and less complicated than those needed for thousands and millions of people.

Adam, Eve, Cain, and Abel worked together as a small group, and their ways of gathering berries (i.e., finding, picking, and eating) constitute social interaction. This small group became a society as its numbers increased. Institutions are society's ways of accomplishing tasks. Put another way, an *institution* is society's rules focused on a long-range need. For instance, society's rules governing how its members are to distribute goods and services is called an *economy*. Another example of an institution is marriage. This governs how large numbers of people select partners.

In sum, a large society needs different methods of functioning than smaller groups do. Standardized ways of dealing with these basic needs are society's institutions.[23]

Social Problems

New forms of social organization materialize as society grows in size. Once, there were clans, and, later, communities, cities, and nation-states. The interests of one segment of society (e.g., upper class) may conflict with those of another sector (e.g., lower class). Conflict and change emerge in society as it evolves.

There are two ways of defining a social problem. One recognizes a condition as a problem when a majority decides it is. For instance, a preponderant number of societal members notice a canning factory dumping waste into a local river. The other approach acknowledges differing viewpoints on a condition as a social problem. Supporters of gun control legislation, for instance, claim the presence of guns in society is a social problem, while members of the National Rifle Association view gun removal from society as a social problem!

Social problems generate from routine operations of society (e.g., creating wealth can foster poverty). They arise from society's efforts to encourage while also causing some to deviate. For example, Americans want to own property. Some people work for it; others steal it because of discrimination. Finally, social problems spawn from a society that creates categories of people, with some having more than others. This creates inequality, and each stratum (e.g., class) defines social problems differently. Therefore, each stratum proposes different solutions for social problems. For instance, an upper-class person may see poverty as a result of lazy people not wanting to work, and so may propose job training to eliminate this condition. People from lower strata may see poverty as a result of the greed of the wealthy, and so may advocate for an equitable distribution of wealth.[24]

Social Change

The narrative started with Adam and Eve in the Garden of Sociology. Out of all possible ways of behaving, they learned, through trial and error, which methods satisfied their needs. Collectively, these methods formed diagrams-for-social-living that provided solutions for solving problems-in-living for them and their offspring. Consequently, these diagrams defined reality for them. For instance, Adam and Eve's diagram-for-social-living distinguished between the chosen and damned people. Hence, their diagram looked like figure 1.3:

Eat apples | Eat blueberries | Eat apples

FIGURE 1.3: Application of the Diagram-for-
Social-Living to Adam and Eve's life.

In the above illustration, the chosen are those who conformed to the normative order. They eat blueberries. The damned are those who eat apples.

New methods of satisfying needs arise as human groups grow. Consequently, their interactions change. Social change is a fundamental transformation occurring over time in the patterns of culture, social structure, and social behavior.[25] In other words, social change describes, as well as brings about, alterations in society's diagrams-for-social-living. The wellspring of social change has many sources: (1) cultural processes (e.g., inventions), (2) societal processes (e.g., modernization), (3) physical processes (e.g., population changes), and (4) human action (e.g., wars).

As we know, society changes over time. It evolved from hunting and gathering to agriculture, to industry. Today, it is a postindustrial or computer/information/service society. Once, people lived in small and homogeneous groups oriented toward the sacred, with a subsistence economy. Today, they occupy large, heterogeneous groups oriented toward the secular and more focused on the material (with a more-than-subsistence economy in the West). The variety of racial, ethnic, and social classes living together generates friction and conflict. Economies that create surpluses generate a consumption-oriented and competitive society. Social change describes this fundamental shift in social living.

The book addresses these questions: Do aliens and the deceased have diagrams-for-social-living? If they do, are they similar or different? What is the similarity and difference that exist between their diagrams and those on Earth?

What Is Other in Other Worlds?

Often, many refer to societies other than their own as *other worlds.*
College students in the United States who study another world (i.e.,
society and culture), probably take an anthropology course, and they
examine how humans congregate into categories, such as tribes and
chiefdoms. While anthropology studies contemporary cultures, its
emphasis is on past and primitive (i.e., limited technology) cultures.[26]
As Raymond Scupin states,

> Anthropologist Morton Fried once pointed out the
> similarities between space travel described in science
> fiction and the field of anthropology. He noted that
> when Neil Armstrong became the first human to set
> foot on the moon in July 1969, his step constituted
> first contact. To space travelers created by science
> fiction writers, *first contact* refers to the first meeting
> between humans and extraterrestrial beings. To
> anthropologists, the phrase refers to initial encounters
> between peoples of different societies.[27]

This book turns Raymond Scupin's interpretation of Morton
Fried's statement on end! It studies worlds found beyond Earth. It
compares and contrasts alien and afterlife worlds with each other and
with contemporary American society. The other worlds in this book
are found in the *ecto* realm.

Levels of Social Living (Up/Down)

Social life[28] can be imagined in terms of size. The smallest unit of
social life is two people, or a *dyad*. The next level is a *triad*, or three
people. Moving up, there are small groups, such as a few friends
having breakfast. Then there are committees, teams (i.e., baseball),
bands (i.e., hunters and gatherers), and tribes (i.e., Aborigines in
Australia). Racial (e.g., white people) and ethnic (e.g., Koreans and

Colombians) groups are further up. The following chart visualizes this ascent.

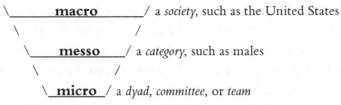

_____ **macro** _____/ a *society*, such as the United States

_____ **messo** ___/ a *category*, such as males

_ **micro** _/ a *dyad, committee,* or *team*

FIGURE 1.4: Levels of Social Living from Micro to Macro.

Social units on the lowest point are in the *micro* level of social life. The *messo* is the middle plane, while the *macro* point is the largest and most complex level of social living. The subject matter in this book is literally off the chart! According to the Merriam-Webster dictionary, *ecto* means "outside" or "external." So, we will be beyond the social life on Earth when we are on the ecto level.

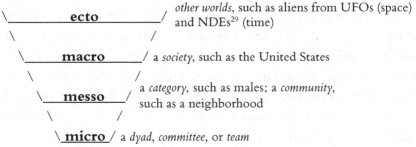

_____ **ecto** _____/ *other worlds*, such as aliens from UFOs (space) and NDEs[29] (time)

_____ **macro** _____/ a *society*, such as the United States

_____ **messo** ___/ a *category*, such as males; a *community*, such as a neighborhood

_ **micro** _/ a *dyad, committee,* or *team*

FIGURE 1.5: Levels of Social Living from Micro to Ecto.

Dimensions of Other Worlds, Space, and Time

The *ecto* level (that is, a dimension beyond Earth's societies) is found in *space* and *time*. Coverage of the UFO experience brings us into outer space, while the treatment of the NDE phenomenon concerns time (i.e., the point after death).

What is being done in the book has *not* been done anywhere. However, astrosociology, founded in 2003 by Dr. Jim Pass, is defined by the Astrosociology Research Institute as "the study of astrosocial phenomena (i.e., the social, cultural, and behavioral patterns related to outer space)."[30] It is the "study of the relationship between 'outer space and society,' and is sometimes referred to as the 'intersection between space exploration and humanity.'"[31] Astrosociology looks at how space exploration affects human beings and their social structures. However, astrosociology does not consider alien beings and their social worlds. This is the subject matter of this book.

No one has studied these phenomena, largely because of the accepted assertion that these realms do not exist. Many see these descriptions as products of science fiction. But, to those who have witnessed them, they are as real as a cold winter's wind blowing in their faces. We do not argue that this wind exists when its blowing makes our own faces tingle. UFO witnesses believe UFOs and aliens are real; so, too, NDErs suppose beings encountered on the other side of life are authentic. They argue that these beings from these other dimensions, unseen by many, are nonetheless real to them; they are as real as a blast of winter's wind on one's face.

I invite you on a journey into space (i.e., outer space) and time (i.e., time after death). Are alien and afterlife worlds structured like societies on Earth? If they are, you will discover that no matter where in time or space intelligent beings are found, they cluster into groups. They work in communal gatherings to solve problems-in-living. In other words, you will discover you have not gone anywhere, but, in fact, have found home.

Let us proceed with the rest of our journey. ...

PART II
OTHER WORLDS

2

UFOS, ALIENS, AND
HUMAN WITNESSES

UFO Defined

What is a UFO? According to J. Allen Hynek, it is:

> The reported perception of an object or light seen in
> the sky or upon the land; the appearance, trajectory,
> and general dynamic and luminescent behavior
> of which do not suggest a logical, conventional
> explanation and which is not only mystifying to the
> original percipients but remains unidentified after
> close scrutiny of all available evidence by persons who
> are technically capable of making a commonsense
> identification, if one is possible.[1]

A UFO is some flying thing witnessed by a human, and it is an
object that defies common sense or earthly explanation.

Another UFO definition is "A flying saucer, an (apparently)
flying object whose nature is unknown; especially those considered to
have extraterrestrial origins."[2] This definition focuses on a particular
and popular perception of a UFO. It is saucer-shaped, and it flies.
However, witnesses describe UFOs in other ways. For example, some

witnesses have described UFOs as cylindrical, rectangular, or discoid, referring to them as shape-shifters and light forms.[3]

In sum, a UFO is an unidentified object usually flying in the sky. No human may be able to give a clear description to it. Thus, *unidentified* does not mean it is not seen. It is, but there is no language sufficient to describe what is observed.

How many UFOs become identified flying objects (i.e., IFOs)? As many as 95 percent of them are identified, while 5 percent remain unidentified. Most UFOs are airplanes seen at different angles.

A History of the UFO Movement in the United States: The Evolution of a Phenomenon

The UFO phenomenon is worldwide and historical. It has been observed on every continent on Earth. These recordings date back to the time of cavemen. Carvings in caves have been described as UFOs. According to Charles Berlitz and William Moore:

> The ancient skies seemed to be filled with aerial travelers. The Assyrians saw flying bulls, ancient Greek and Arabs saw flying horses, the opulent Persians thought they saw flying carpets, the warlike Romans watched flying shields and spears and whole battles in the sky at the very moment that they themselves were engaged in earthly combat.

> As the ancient world became Christianized, the aerial sightings became fiery crosses and other threatening signs of doom foretelling plagues and disasters. The Emperor Constantine of Byzantium saw something in the sky before a battle that convinced him to become a Christian, considerably changing thereby the course of history.

When the Renaissance opened up people's minds to the exploration of the world, UFOs appropriately took the form of galleys and caravels, and then, as the French first began experimenting with balloons, certain vast globes were seen floating in the upper heavens, almost as monstrous reflections of what the French were doing. Starting in the late 1800s, relatively modern observers have described UFOs as flying spindles, cigars, and then airships moving at tremendous speeds. In World Wars I and II they were taken to be some sort of unexplained weapon (World War II: "foo fighters") which each side thought the other was using. ... [4]

The number of sightings, and, more recently, of abductions is overwhelming. A Google search reveals thousands of websites with such data. This text focuses on only sightings in the United States.

The UFO phenomenon in the United States started in earnest in 1947, with two significant events. The first happened in the skies above Washington state, while the second took place on the ground in New Mexico. These occurrences happened nine days apart!

On June 24, 1947, Kenneth Arnold of Boise, Idaho, was flying his private plane near Mount Rainier in Washington. He saw nine silvery objects traveling very fast outside of his window. After he landed, he reported what he had observed. The next day, Arnold was interviewed by Bill Bequette of the Associated Press (AP). When Bequette asked Arnold what he saw, he replied, "A saucer skipping over water."[5] Bequette sent his report to the AP and coined the phrase *flying saucer.* The phrase took hold, and a phenomenon began.

The second defining moment in UFO history in the United States began on July 2, 1947. Allegedly, a flying saucer crashed on the Foster Ranch near Corona, New Mexico. (The crash site was identified by the larger town in the area, Roswell.) Debris scattered along a half-mile path. On July 3, William "Mac" Brazel and his seven-year-old neighbor, Dee Proctor, found parts tossed on the ground. Brazel drove Dee home and showed an item to Dee's parents (Floyd and Loretta).

25

They said the pieces looked very unusual. Three days later (July 6), Mac showed a piece of wreckage to the county sheriff, George Wilcox. He contacted Major Jesse Marcel at Roswell Army Air Force Field. The major, an intelligence officer, went to the site and reported his findings to Colonel William "Butch" Blanchard.[6] The colonel held a press conference and announced finding a UFO. General Roger Ramey heard about Blanchard's press conference and ordered him to (1) fly the wreckage to Wright-Patterson Air Force Base (AFB) in Dayton, Ohio; and (2) to hold a second press conference denying the UFO. Consequently, Blanchard claimed they found a "weather balloon."[7]

Many believed the follow-up story, but it contained discrepancies that confused people. The Roswell incident then went dormant for thirty years.

The general public forgot the incident, but not the United States Air Force (USAF). A confluence of factors led the USAF into a series of investigations. They were (1) the need to correct the poor way the USAF handled the incident; (2) the wish to avoid negative public attention by the national press; (3) the necessity to acquire information about a widespread phenomenon; and (4) the potential threat to US security.

Collectively, these reports are Project Blue Book. The project started in 1947 and ended twenty-two years later, in 1969. The USAF was the unit that investigated UFOs. Project Blue Book was not well funded and not competently staffed.[8]

The USAF's investigation of UFOs started at the Wright-Patterson AFB in Ohio, on June 30, 1947.[9] It did not have an official name when it began. On January 26, 1948, this activity was named Project Sign. Later, on February 12, 1949, it changed to Project Grudge. Finally, on March 25, 1952, it became Project Blue Book.[10] These changes are documented in the following:

USAF UFO Study Name	Starting Date
Unnamed	June 30, 1947
Project Sign	January 26, 1948
Project Grudge	February 12, 1949

Project Blue Book   March 25, 1952

USAF investigations end   December 17, 1969

The events of that time provide a context for understanding the UFO phenomenon. The Cold War was heating up. The democratic government and capitalistic economic system of the United States was in mortal combat with communistic and socialistic Russia. Neither side trusted the other, and each side aimed thousands of nuclear weapons at the other.

In July 1952, many people sighted several UFOs over Washington, DC. The USAF sent planes to intercept them, but these strange craft were too fast for the air force. People were frightened by these strange, fast, and unknown aircraft.

The US government and military had concerns when many UFO reports arrived from around the country. Many questions were raised. Do these entities exist? What are their origins? Are they a threat to the United States? The army chief of staff, Lt. Gen. Nathan Twining, sent a letter to the commanding general of the army air force. He claimed the UFO phenomenon was real, and it needed to be investigated.[11] In late 1947, the government created Project Sign. Project members concluded UFOs were real, and they had an extraterrestrial origin. Their superiors did not buy their explanation. The project ended.

The USAF took data from the defunct Project Sign and started Project Grudge (1949–52). Project Blue Book "was created under Project Sign . . . which evolved into Project Grudge."[12] It lasted twenty-two years and ended on December 17, 1969. Of the 12,618 UFO sightings recorded during this time, 701 remained unidentified.[13] This represented almost 6 percent of the total. Today, individual sightings are arranged chronologically in the National Archives, in a space of approximately thirty-seven cubic feet.[14]

UFO investigations discontinued as a result of (1) an evaluation of a report from the University of Colorado entitled, *Scientific Study of Unidentified Flying Objects*; (2) a review of the university's report by the National Academy of Sciences; (3) past UFO studies; and (4) USAF experience investigating UFO reports during the 1940s, 1950s, and

1960s. Investigators attached to Project Blue Book concluded that (1) UFOs never presented a threat to US security;[15] (2) no evidence given to the USAF indicated UFOs represented technological developments or principles beyond present-day scientific knowledge; and (3) no evidence indicated unidentified vehicles were extraterrestrial.[16]

On February 21, 1978, Jesse Marcel contacted Stanton Friedman, a reputable ufologist (i.e., expert on UFOs; Marcel was the first federal official contacted after the Roswell crash). Marcel told Friedman his Roswell story, but it was not presented coherently. Consequently, Friedman abandoned Marcel's story. One year later, William Moore found a clipping describing what Marcel told Friedman. Moore contacted Friedman, and his interest was sparked once again.

The Roswell story gained legitimacy because Friedman was well respected in the UFO community. Consequently, a larger audience received it. Sixty-three years later, the Roswell incident is celebrated in writing and folklore. The site is a "holy place" for those interested in ufology.[17]

In a general way, UFO history began in the United States with the above-mentioned events. Since Kenneth Arnold's observation and the Roswell incident, there have been thousands of reports of sightings and human abductions. All of these data suggest a pattern of activity spanning from the 1940s to today. In the 1940s and 1950s, the general population saw UFO craft. In the late 1950s and early 1960s, humans saw a variety of alien beings. In the late 1960s and into the 1970s, aliens made contact. Later, Steven Spielberg's films, such as *Close Encounters of the Third Kind* (1977) and *E.T. the Extra-Terrestrial* (1982), immortalized these events.

A significant shift in the UFO phenomenon started in the 1980s. Not only did humans see aliens and have contact with them, the aliens took the humans! Humans reported missing time and being abducted. People said that aliens examined them aboard spacecraft. Every orifice of their bodies received probes and prods. In the beginning of these ministrations, the purpose of these exams seemed to be acquisition of knowledge. This was much like information humans gained with similar procedures when they tagged dolphins and other earthly creatures. Later, the purpose for these intrusive procedures escalated. Aliens extracted sperm from human men and eggs from human women. More recently, they had sexual intercourse with humans (both male and female). People described these encounters as involuntary, but, on occasion, they were voluntary!

The UFO/alien phenomenon has grown since the 1940s. A reality about them has been actively constructed. First, Stanton Friedman publicized it through lectures and articles. In a real sense, his actions legitimized this phenomenon—at least it did among UFO believers. The story evolved from merely seeing strange flying objects to observing their landing, followed by creatures stepping out of these flying objects and contacting humans. People and their alien lovers now agree on intimacies of an extraordinary kind!

Methodology: How Were Data Selected for Describing UFOs and Aliens?

Information about UFOs and aliens is overwhelming. For instance, a Google search of UFOs, aliens, and UFOs and aliens yielded 23.5 million, 168 million, and 11.7 million hits, respectively. It is impossible to review all of these sources. A sample is needed.

Material about UFOs and aliens comes from two sources. The first is the On This Day databank compiled by Donald A. Johnson.[18] This information appears throughout this chapter. Wendelle C. Stevens's books[19] provide the second source of information (explored in chapter 3).

The On This Day databank organized reports of people from around the world who either saw a UFO or had an alien contact. Arranged into a calendar from January 1 to December 31, it recorded each date that a human observed a UFO and/or alien and then submitted that observation to the databank.

Usually, a date had twenty or more cases. Each case listed (1) who saw the UFO and/or alien (these individuals were called "witnesses"); additionally, (2) the databank recorded the time of day of a sighting; and (3) a short description of the observation. These reports spanned from the 1800s to the present time.

As of April 2012, this databank had 7,144 cases. As it was impossible to secure information from all of them, two samples were drawn about one year apart (i.e., 2011 and 2012). The first sample had 835 cases, while the second had 821, for a total of 1,656 unduplicated cases. I selected every eighth case in the 2011 sample and every tenth case in 2012; I discarded duplicate cases. The combined samples represented about 23 percent of the entire population.[20]

Most of the cases found in the On This Day database recorded ET sightings, usually of UFOs but also, on occasion, alien beings. In the rarest of cases, these aliens spoke to humans, and their messages were documented in the databank. Because most of these data focused on UFO craft, most of what the database noted was the material aspect of alien culture. In those rare instances when aliens were described, I created a demographic portrait of them, complete with the characteristics of their population (i.e., age, sex, and race).

Basic Information about UFOs and Aliens

There are five fundamental questions about UFOs and aliens. They are identified in the box below.

---

1. Who are the aliens coming to Earth? Who are the humans seeing them?
2. What are the characteristics of UFOs?
3. When are UFOs and aliens seen? Are there specific years, months, and hours when they are seen?
4. Where are UFOs and aliens seen? Are they seen worldwide?
5. Why do aliens come to Earth? Do they have messages for humans?

A Demographic[21] Portrait of Aliens and UFOs

Aliens: Who Occupies UFOs?

I examined who aliens were. In the first sample,[22] there were 835 cases. Only 186 of them had enough information to adequately describe alien characteristics. This represented about 22 percent of the sample. The second sample contained 821 cases. Two hundred cases (or 24 percent of sample two) had sufficient information.

What follows is a thorough description of aliens. This section identifies alien height, sex, race, and physical characteristics such as head shape.

Height

The height of aliens presented two problems. First, several cases identified alien height as "tall" and "dwarfish." These cases were vague and therefore omitted. For instance, how tall is "tall"? The information given was not precise. What is tall to one person may not be to another. Second, some occasions identified alien height in such a range as three and a half feet to four feet. These cases were indefinite and therefore dropped. The problem was how to make a determination.

Sample one had sixty-two cases with a sufficient amount of information to determine the precise height of an alien. Sample two had forty-three cases. Table 2.1 lists the variety of alien heights.

Table 2.1: An Identification of Alien Height

	Sample #1	Sample #2
Range:	from 2" to 13'2"	from 31" to 9'
Mean/Average:	5'2"	5'1"
Median:	5'	5'
Mode:	6'	4'

As table 2.1 shows, the range of heights in the two samples was similar. The size of aliens extended from inches to feet. The range of heights was wider in the first sample than in the second (i.e., two inches to thirteen feet, two inches versus thirty-one inches to nine feet). In some cases, one could step on an alien as if it were a mouse because some aliens were only two inches tall. On other occasions, one could consider an alien's height to be comparable to a dog's, as some aliens were thirty-one inches tall. Other aliens were far taller. Anyone who came upon an alien nine feet tall—or thirteen feet, two inches tall—would surely be frightened by such a giant!

The average size of an alien was virtually the same in both samples (i.e., five feet, two inches versus five feet, one inch). The median[23] was exactly the same (i.e., five feet). The mode[24] was six feet tall in sample one and four feet tall in sample two. Overall, a typical alien was about five feet tall, while a normal adult human is, on average, between five feet and six feet tall.[25] Therefore, aliens resemble humans, at least in height.

Sex

Apparently, there are only males and females in the universe, as on Earth.[26] Of the 186 alien cases in sample one, only twenty-eight of them identified the alien's sex. The alien cases in sample two had forty such instances.

An alien's sex was rarely determined. Why? There were many reasons. Often, aliens were simply not seen during a UFO incident. If they were, it was from a distance and therefore difficult to see their bodies. Also, their spacecraft shielded their bodies. Moreover, aliens wore clothing, which made it difficult to ascertain their sex. Additionally, humans viewed these occurrences briefly and under duress.

In situations where aliens' sex was identified, by far, most of them were males. (See table 2.2.)

Table 2.2: Documentation of Aliens' Sex

# of Cases Involving	Sample #1	Sample #2	Total:
Only male aliens:	21	37	58

Only female aliens:	4	2	6
Males and females:	<u>3</u>	<u>1</u>	<u>4</u>
Total:	**28**	**40**	**68**

There were occasions when females accompanied their male counterparts, but these were rare occurrences. Presumably, alien space travelers, like human space crews, were overwhelmingly male. Apparently, cosmic traveling is predominantly a male activity, whether your home planet is Earth or anywhere else in the universe!

Race

Seemingly, aliens were like humans. Both recognized races within their species.[27] Presumably, their skin color, like that of humans, took shape as an adaptation to their environment. In the two samples, witnesses identified an alien's color as "dark," "pale," or "fair." In a couple of cases, humans described aliens as "Oriental-looking." I put pale and fair aliens seen by witnesses in the *white* category. I placed dark aliens into the *black* category. These inclusions fit conventional earthly racial categories.[28]

Using a continuum of colors ranging from light to dark, I identified alien races in the following manner:

LIGHT-White-Pale-Fair-Pink-Gray-Yellowish-
Reddish-Orange-Tan-Bronze-Brown-Blue-Olive-
Green-Black-**DARK**

The races of aliens are summarized in table 2.3.

Table 2.3: A Description of Alien Races

	# of Aliens with this Color	
	Sample #1	**Sample #2**
An Alien's Color/Race:		
White (including pale, fair, pinkish, pink, and white/grayish)	9	4

Gray (sometimes spelled *grey*)	9	7
Black (including *dark*)	4	2
Tan	1	-
Bronze	1	-
Brown (*dark*)	1	-
Olive Skin	1	1
Green	1	3
Reddish/Orange	-	1
Crimson	-	1
Bluish	-	1
Yellowish ("Oriental-looking")	1	2
Total:	**28**	**22**

Witnesses seldom identified an alien's race. When they did, they said aliens were gray or white. Together, these colors accounted for twenty-nine out of fifty cases. Classification of beings by race was tricky business. On Earth, humans created five races (i.e., black, white, red, yellow, and brown), but placing them into these categories is often difficult. Some have characteristics that are hard to catalog. For instance, where does one place people of mixed races? For example, it may be easy to classify former President Bill Clinton into the white race, but it is more difficult to place President Barack Obama into a category because he is mixed-race.

One may ask, "How do we account for the variety of colors among aliens as compared to humans?" I identified about sixteen different alien colors. They included such colors as blue, green, and crimson. How can one account for these differences? Do aliens come from different planets with diverse environmental conditions that create a wide array of skin colors? Do aliens come from the same planet but with unalike environmental surroundings that create a variety of skin colors? For example, on Earth, people native to the northern hemisphere tend to have lighter complexions, while those native to the southern hemisphere tend to have darker complexions. We do not have enough information about alien races to form an opinion as to the reason for skin color.

Physical Characteristics of Aliens

What does an alien look like? Alien bodies are described from head to toe in table 2.4. I selected three of these attributes (head shape, eyes, and fingers/claws/wrists/hands) to comment on in detail in this section. I also included alien movements and sounds in this section, although these are not listed in table 2.4.

I compiled a picture of alien characteristics from the On This Day databank. The first sample was drawn in 2011, and the second sample was pulled in 2012. Two samples were selected for comparison purposes.

Table 2.4: A Record of Alien Body shapes and Other Characteristics

	# of Times Mentioned	
<u>Physical Characteristics:</u>	<u>Sample #1</u>	<u>Sample #2</u>
Body Shape	84	49
Eyes	49	45
Head Shape	38	35
Hair	34	23
Arms	21	24
Fingers/Claws/Wrists/Hands	15	9
Mouth	12	11
Legs/Knees/Ankles/Feet/Toes	10	12
Nose	7	13
Ears	7	10

Alien Head Shape

(Sample one) By far, the most common description of an alien head was "large" or "oversized." Only twice was an alien's head termed "small," and, in one of those cases, it was further described as being "like a doorknob set in between its shoulders."[29] Alien heads were egg- or pear-shaped, and sometimes bald. On occasion, witnesses reported protrusions emanating from an alien's head.

(Sample two) Again, the most often-mentioned characterization of alien heads was the size. In fourteen cases, the alien's head was described as "large" or "oversized" (as in sample one). One witness deemed an alien's head was "half its height." Another witness said an alien's head was "very small." People described alien heads as round, elongated, square, and lemon-shaped. Twice, they mentioned the color of an alien's head: grayish or blackish-gray. Finally, these individuals reported vapor or tentacles protruding from the head.

Alien Eyes

(Sample one) Observers reported the following about alien eyes. (1) They were larger than human eyes; (2) they were asymmetrical, narrow, and "Oriental-looking" (some observers said alien eyes looked like "round holes in the place of eyes"); and (3) alien eye colors ranged from fierce, glowing red to penetrating blue.

(Sample two) Witnesses reported that (1) the size of alien eyes was large; (2) the shape was round or slanted; and (3) the eye color ranged from yellow to black. In one case, a witness reported an alien had "a cyclops eye floating to the ground"!

Alien Fingers/Claws/Wrists/Hands

(Sample one) Most often witnesses reported hands and fingers. They observed them "in a praying position" or "raised" above an alien's head. These creatures' hands had three, four, or six fingers, although some had no fingers or nails. One witness mentioned a wrist, and two noted claws.

(Sample two) Individuals noted the presence of hands, which sometimes appeared greenish, rugged, or normal. They depicted them as pincerlike or clawlike. Some saw three or four fingers on a hand, and one saw "eight talon-like fingers."

Alien Movements and Sounds

(Sample one) Witnesses saw aliens moving far more often than they heard them making sounds or communicating. In sample one, there were twenty-nine cases in which witnesses saw aliens move, heard them talk or make noises. In eight of these cases, sounds were heard.

(Sample two) In this sample, there were 153 cases where witnesses observed aliens engaged in some form of action, but they only heard them in twenty-six of these cases.

The disparity between seeing aliens in action or hearing them may be a function of the type of cases reported to the On This Day databank. Most of the cases recorded in this databank are not examples of close encounters of the fourth kind (i.e., CE-IV). This type of encounter involves personal contact between aliens and humans, the most dramatic of which is alien abduction of humans. The On This Day database recorded more observations of aliens by humans than "up close and personal" contact with them.

It was difficult categorizing alien movements because they were so diverse. Witnesses observed creatures walking, standing, or floating. Sometimes they moved slowly, while at other times they went quickly. On occasion, they were motionless, flew, glided, or descended. They squatted, leaped, or simply moved. One person reported an alien that performed somersaults on wet grass! Aliens walked mechanically, were stiff-legged, or had a limp. In addition to ambulating, aliens moved their body parts. In one case, an alien "seemed to move its arms around," while in another instance, "they rocked their torsos slowly back and forth."

In addition to ambulation, alien movements involved actions. Oftentimes observers watched aliens fixing their spacecraft. These people witnessed creatures drinking from a pond and performing a medical procedure. Once, someone saw an alien entering a restaurant and ordering chicken with plenty of red pepper and powdered saffron!

Sometimes alien movements were threatening. For instance, an alien pointed a beam at a witness in bed, while another approached a witness and touched him on the arm, burning him. An alien immobilized a police officer with a luminous ray. Sometimes alien aggression was focused on themselves. In one incident aliens struggled together.

Although rarely reported, there were occasions when aliens made sounds. They made "sizzling sounds," "noises sounding like rain on a drainpipe," and "strange clicking noises." The creatures sounded "guttural," "talked mechanically," and had a "chirping voice."

What Are Some Material Items of Alien Culture?

Alien apparel was described by style, color, material composition, function, and accessories. Sample one had ninety-four cases describing alien dress. In sample two, there were ninety-five such cases.

What Was the Style of Alien Clothes?

In sample one, seventy-eight cases answered the above question, while in sample two, fifty-eight cases answered the question. The style of alien clothes is found in table 2.5.

Table 2.5: Type of Apparel Worn by Aliens

	# of Times Mentioned	
Type/Style of Garments:	Sample #1	Sample #2
Suit	21	14
Coveralls, overalls	9	14
Uniform	9	2
Outfits	8	3
Clothing	7	7
Garments	3	0
Tunic	3	0
Gown	2	0
Jacket	2	1
Shirt	2	1
Cape, coat, habit	1 (each)	0 (each)
Jeans, trousers, or pants (alone)	0	3

Jeans and shirt	1	2
Pants and jacket	1	1
Parka-like/hooded	1	0

By far, in both samples, aliens wore suits. These suits could be "flight suits" or "diving suits,"[30] as described in sample one; or, "shiny and metallic," as portrayed in sample two. It was possible that suits served as protective gear. Coveralls and overalls were also worn as protective gear, but these served as work clothes as well. Perhaps aliens wore them for excavating UFO debris after a crash. Frequently, alien garments were described as "tight-fitted." In one case, a witness took note of the "musculature" of an alien's body.

Perhaps it is necessary to broaden our understanding about how aliens dressed. In addition to protecting them from a harsh environment, and wearing them as uniforms, maybe there is a third purpose for their clothing. It is possible that aliens dressed in such ways to seduce humans! In some recent books depicting alien abduction of persons, humans have both involuntarily and voluntarily had sex with aliens![31]

What Color Were Alien Clothes?

I present a description of the color of alien apparel. These accounts are found in table 2.6.

Table 2.6: Identification of Color in Alien Apparel

	# of Times Mentioned	
Color of Alien Garments:	Sample #1	Sample #2
Silver/Silvery	14	7
White	11	4
Black	8	7
Blue	6	5
Gray	6	6

Yellow	5	0
Red	4	2
Green	3	4
Brown	2	2
Pale Cream	1	0
Shiny	1	7

(Sample one) In this sample, most witnesses described aliens' garments with these colors: silver, white, black, blue, or gray.

(Sample two) In this sample, most witnesses described aliens' garments as being silver, black, or shiny (no color given with "shiny").

The color of alien apparel was similar in both samples, but their proportions were uneven. This may be a function of what witnesses saw or what they reported. More data would be required to draw a logical conclusion.

When an alien's garment was silver or silvery, it could also be "shiny" or "glowing" in the first sample, as compared to "luminescent" in sample two. In sample one, witnesses described trousers color as white in two cases, and luminous and silvery in two other cases. In sample two, witnesses used white to describe spacesuits, uniforms, or cassocks/smocks. Black, light blue-gray, and blue were colors frequently mentioned in both samples. Either aliens were totally dressed in blue, or part of their outfit was this color.

In both samples, witnesses saw six examples of gray apparel. This gray color could be two-toned or dark in sample one, or metallic in sample two.

What Materials Comprised Alien Clothes?

Samples one and two had few references describing the composition of alien clothes. Some parts of alien apparel, such as suits and helmets, were made of plastic and metal. For instance, in sample one, a shield over an alien's eyes was made of plastic, while in sample two, a suit was metallic. In sample two, clothes were reported as "resembling bright armor"; whereas in sample one, witnesses saw "two rubber suits" and "a glass fishbowl-type helmet." Witnesses saw leather in both samples. In the first, it was a belt; in the second, pants.

What Part of an Alien's Body Was Covered by Clothes?

In most cases, alien apparel was mentioned specifically, and the part of the body covered was inferred. For instance, when a witness said he saw an alien with trousers, it was assumed that these pants covered the alien's legs. Pants, helmets, shirts, jackets, and gowns were cited, indicating that alien legs, heads, and torsos were covered. From these descriptions, aliens seemed to be like everyday humans. Some of their apparel might be considered deviant. For instance, when an alien wore a "glass fishbowl-like helmet," most humans would consider it odd.

What Were Alien Accessories?

In both samples, about half the aliens had accessories, with helmets the most often-mentioned. Many helmets had things attached to them, such as visors and antennae. These helmets were round, square, and translucent. Also, aliens carried many objects, such as a box that was strapped to the chest. In another example, a creature carried a box under its arms. A witness thought that this device would assist in the alien's ascent into its spacecraft.

In addition to boxes, individuals reported that aliens held torches. One witness described an alien that wore "a miner's hat." Aliens wore head caps, berets, gloves, and hoods. Some aliens carried implements and instruments. In one case, a witness recounted a boxlike implement that an alien pointed at him. In another incident, an alien held a pear-shaped instrument that glowed. Other accessories, such as a laser gun and a .357 pistol, had more potency.

Apparently, their accessories helped aliens navigate severe environments, provided techniques for conducting experiments, and offered them protection against potentially hostile humans. Clearly, aliens possessed a wealth of material items of culture to sustain them in their space travels.

A Demographic Portrait of Witnesses

Our next examination describes the characteristics of witnesses. Who saw UFOs and aliens? What were their social characteristics (i.e., age, sex, and race)?

How Old Were Witnesses?

There were a good number of witnesses in the 1,656 sample cases, but their exact ages were difficult to determine. Often, a witness's age was identified with indeterminate language, such as "child," "high school age," and "middle-aged." Exactly how old was a middle-aged person, for instance? Table 2.7 lists the ages of witnesses found in the samples.

Table 2.7: The Range of Witnesses' Ages

Years Old:	1st Sample		2nd Sample		Total
0–9:	3	+	7	=	10
10–19:	36		29		65
20–29:	25		12		37
30–39:	5		13		18
40–49:	8		13		21
50–59:	4		2		6
60–69:	4		3		7
70–79:	1		1		2
80+:	=		1		1
Total:	86		81		167

For those with specific ages, a little over 67 percent were younger than thirty years of age. Of these, most were between ten and nineteen years old. Only roughly 6 percent were sixty years of age or older.

What Were the Sexes of Witnesses?

There were many cases in both samples where determining the sex of a witness was difficult. For instance, one witness was identified as a pilot. One may summarize that this individual was a male, but it could have been a female. Also, some references were not English names, making it difficult to determine the sex of these individuals. In other instances, the sex of a witness was not mentioned.

Table 2.8 identifies the sex of human witnesses.

Table 2.8: Identification of the Sex of Witnesses

Sex:	Sample #1	Sample #2	Total
Male:	432	326	758
Female:	147	169	316

Table 2.8 shows that there were far more male witnesses than female. In both samples, male witnesses outnumbered female witnesses. The margin was more than 2 to 1.

What Were Witnesses' Occupations?

Witnesses' occupations fell into seven categories, listed alphabetically, below:

1. Education worker/teacher
2. Government worker/ member of military
3. Professional (nonreligious)/ member of clergy
4. Scientist
5. Service worker
6. Skilled worker
7. Unskilled worker

These occupations are found in table A.1 in appendix A. Witnesses represented every walk of life. They were found in eighty-one different occupations. Among them were skilled and unskilled workers, such as meteorological observer and grocery worker. There were ministers and members of the military. A golfing pro and a US senator were listed among the witnesses.[32]

What can be learned from the witnesses' occupations? Aliens wished to contact every type of human being in order to spread their (aliens') message; or, aliens wished to know about the diversity of Earth's people. Perhaps they intended both outcomes.

Characteristics of UFOs

What did the UFOs observed by witnesses look like? UFOs were described by type, size, shape, composition, color, lights, movements, sounds, and speed.

What Type of Objects Did People See?

Most people described UFOs as disc-shaped. They were usually seen in the sky, but frequently were viewed on Earth. *UFO* often referred to the vehicles aliens used for transportation. This term can also describe any unidentified flying object. For instance, lights and balls of energy could be UFOs too. The descriptions that follow apply to alien transports.

What Size Were UFOs?

Most UFOs were small (i.e., less than one hundred cubic feet). The average dimensions were thirty-four to thirty-seven feet long by thirty-four to thirty-seven feet wide by six and a half feet high. Other UFOs were large: "the size of a car," "six miles in diameter," and "half the size of the moon."

What Shape Were UFOs?

Among the descriptions given by witnesses were "a [flying] saucer," "two plates, rim-to-rim," "domed," "triangular," "boomerang-shaped," "cigar-like," "oval," and "a stealth fighter with rounded wings."

What Materials Composed UFOs?

Mostly, they were metallic. In one instance, a human shot bullets from a rifle at a UFO. They ricocheted, making a sound of bullets hitting metal.

What Color Were UFOs?

Witnesses reported a variety of colors, among them shades of silver, gray, blue, orange, red, and green. Sometimes witnesses said parts of UFOs were different colors. For instance, the underside of a UFO was described as dark, while the rest of it was very bright. Also, a UFO's color could change. For instance, one was seen to change from yellow-green to yellow-white before ascending. Another was observed as aluminum-colored when flying in the sky, but it turned a dull shade of copper when it landed. One can speculate that a UFO's changes in color corresponded to changes in its speed, direction, and landing. For example, a witness saw one UFO glow and then dim. Perhaps aliens change the color of UFOs as a camouflage to fit into Earth's terrain.

Lights were seen both on UFOs and independent of them. When they were seen on a UFO, they sometimes functioned as warning lights (like on airplanes). At other times, lights seemed to be connected to how a UFO flew. Lights changed colors when a UFO ascended, descended, or increased its speed. When not attached to a UFO, lights were seen as a ball on the ground. Sometimes the light was a beam from a UFO or something unknown.

Observers saw lights emanating from inside UFOs. Some people viewed this light from the ground looking up into the windows of UFOs. Others saw this light while inside a spacecraft. Those outside saw the light as blue, while those inside saw it as white.

What follows is a description of alien lights that were outside of a UFO. In some cases, the lights functioned as beams that aided ETs in entering and exiting a craft. Sometimes a light served as a hiding place for ETs while on Earth. For instance, the light/hiding place could be employed to escape an aggressive human. At other times, lights moved slightly above the ground or were seen high in the sky. Lights near the ground were used to cause a change in a human. For example, they dazed a human, making him or her forget; or, they stopped a human's car.

What Kinds of Movements Did UFOs Make?

UFOs and other objects moved in ways that were quite similar. Both demonstrated extreme speeds. Both were very maneuverable. Witnesses saw them moving fast and slow, or stopping in the sky or just above the ground. They zigzagged, remained stationary in the sky, or fell "like a leaf."

Do UFOs Make Sounds?

Sometimes these craft made sounds, and sometimes they did not. Many large and small UFOs made no noticeable sounds. These craft hovered or flew close to an observer. Witnesses heard some sounds. Among them were whirling, whining, humming, and sizzling noises. Claims of dull roaring sounds and shrilling beeping ones have been reported.

How Fast Do UFOs Travel?

Once more, the answers varied. UFOs were observed traveling between 400 and 39,000 miles per hour. One object was listed as going 15 miles per hour, while another moved 1,500 miles per hour.

How can an observer judge a UFO's speed? While some witnesses were pilots, most were civilians who made "guesstimates." Thus, the reliability of these numbers was highly questionable. At best, these witnesses noted UFOs flew very fast, very slow, or stopped dead in the air; that is, they flew at speeds and maneuvered in ways most humans had never seen and could not comprehend.

When Are UFOs Seen?

In What Years Were UFOs Seen?

Data from table B.1 in appendix B showed most sightings occurred in the 1970s, 1960s, and 1950s, respectively. Together, these three decades accounted for more than 70 percent of the reported cases in the last century. Although there was a decline of reported cases in the 1980s, the number increased in the 1990s. Finally, there were only thirteen cases reported before 1900 and 112 cases after 2000.

How Many Sightings Occurred in Each Month?

In table 2.9, you will find the sighting of a UFO by month.

Table 2.9: Month UFOs Were Sighted

MONTH:	SAMPLE #1	SAMPLE #2	TOTAL
January	51	61	**112**
February	50	62	**112**
March	64	64	**128**
April	70	41	**111**
May	62	40	**102**
June	72	64	**136**
July	97	100	**197**
August	86	88	**174**
September	70	71	**141**
October	96	96	**192**
November	56	68	**124**
December	61	66	**127**
Total:	**835**	**821**	**1,656**

The top three months having the most sightings were July, October, and August, respectively. Most sightings happened in North America and Europe, which are in the northern hemisphere. Consequently, it was not surprising to learn that summer and autumn months when people are outside, accounted for most sightings. The months with the fewest sightings were January, February, April, and May. Two of them were in the dead of winter when most northern hemisphere people stay indoors.

During What Hours of the Day Do People See Aliens and UFOs?

In table 2.10, you will find the sighting of a UFO by hour.

Table 2.10: The Hour Aliens and/or UFOs Were Sighted

TIME OF DAY:	SAMPLE #1	+ SAMPLE #2	= TOTAL
Midnight to 2:59 a.m.	84	90	174
3:00 to 5:59 a.m.	64	63	127
6:00 to 8:59 a.m.	25	41	66
9:00 to 11:59 a.m.	33	39	72
Noon to 2:59 p.m.	41	35	76
3:00 to 5:59 p.m.	46	60	106
6:00 to 8:59 p.m.	115	156	271
9:00 to 11:59 p.m.	<u>194</u>	<u>181</u>	<u>375</u>
Total:	**602**	**665**	**1,267**

The data indicated most sightings were between 9:00 p.m. and 12:00 a.m. (midnight). This time frame accounted for nearly 30 percent of the total. The least number of sightings occurred between 6:00 a.m. and 9:00 a.m., in sample one. In sample two, the fewest sightings happened between 12:00 p.m. (noon) and 3:00 p.m.

Most of the reported sightings transpired in the northern hemisphere. It was not surprising that most of them ensued after 9:00 p.m., when most people were home from work. The fewest sightings happened when people were at work.

Where Were UFOs Seen?

The region of the world, country, and US state in which sightings happened was identified in tables C.1, C.2, and C.3, respectively. These tables are found in appendix C.

What Regions of the World Saw UFOs? (See table C.1 in appendix C)

I combined samples one and two, excluding duplicates and listing six world regions: Africa, Asia, Europe, North America, Oceania, and South America. There were 1,764 cases of UFO/alien sightings in these regions. The most transpired in North America, with Europe ranking second, and South America ranking third. Overwhelmingly, sightings were a North American and European experience, in terms of areas where sightings occurred. This may be due to reporting. These regions may have more UFO organizations and staff to report this phenomenon than do other areas of the world. More research is needed to determine this conclusively.

Were There Only Certain Countries Where UFOs Were Seen? (See table C.2 in appendix C)

Seventy-eight countries reported UFO and/or alien sightings. An additional ten sightings were seen in an ocean or on land (e.g., Central Europe). Clearly, the UFO/alien phenomenon was worldwide; however, it was *not* a phenomenon seen evenly throughout the globe. The countries with most reported cases appear below:

2011 Sample:		**2012 Sample:**	
1. United States	393	1. United States	437
2. France	97	2. France	84
3. Australia	44	3. Canada	50

Regional patterns were replicated in the country data. Again, North American and European countries had the most and second-most sightings, respectively. It is open to conjecture as to why this is the case.

What US States Reported UFO/Alien Sightings?
(See table C.3 in appendix C)

The states with the most sightings (in descending order) in each sample and in the combined sample were as follows:

Sample #1:		Sample #2:		Combined Sample:	
1. California	31	1. California	39	1. California	70
2. Massachusetts and Texas	22, each	2. Ohio	36	2. Ohio	55
3. Florida and Illinois	20, each	3. Florida	24	3. Texas	43

Without a doubt, California had the most sightings in both samples, and, consequently, in the combined sample. Out of the five most-populous American states (i.e., California, Texas, New York, Florida, and Illinois [in descending order of size of population]), three of them had the largest number of sightings (i.e., California, Texas, and Florida). Is it simply that there were more people in these states to view and/or report sightings? Every state in sample two had sightings; there were six states in sample one with no sightings (i.e., Alabama, Arkansas, Delaware, Hawaii, Oklahoma, and Vermont). When the samples were combined, every state (and the District of Columbia) had at least one sighting. In the combined sample, ten states had half of all the sightings. They were (in descending order of frequency of sightings):

1. California	70	6. Massachusetts	37
2. Ohio	55	7. Illinois	33
3. Florida	44	8. Pennsylvania	33
4. Texas	42	9. Michigan	29
5. New York	41	10. Washington	25

Total: 409/822 (49.7 percent)

Why Do Aliens Come to Earth?

On the rarest of occasions, aliens spoke to humans. Often, these communications were done through telepathy. Witnesses claimed aliens spoke languages, such as "a mixture of Spanish and English" or an "unintelligible language with a digital musical quality."

What Did Aliens Say to Humans?

Did aliens tell humans where they came from and how they arrived? Did they have a message for humans? Did aliens tell humans how to cure diseases and how to live forever? Did they provide insight into God's existence? Did aliens know where heaven could be found?

In samples one and two, there were only thirty and twenty-five cases, respectively, citing comprehensible information from aliens. Rarely did aliens speak to humans. These alien communications spanned from 1950 to 2006. Most cases occurred in the 1970s.

Most of these communications were commands, requests, reassurances, and dissemination of information. Witnesses said they were told "to sit in a chair," "remain still," and/or not to take "photographs." Sometimes aliens made requests of humans, such as asking a teacher "to go with them," or asking for "water." Most often, aliens reassured people. Witnesses reported that aliens said such things as "Don't be afraid; nothing bad will happen to you." Another witness recounted an alien said, "Not here to harm you but to view you and observe you (humans)." Also, aliens gave information to humans. For instance, a witness claimed an alien said, "I'm going to regenerate you by a procedure that is not yet known on your planet."

Where Did Aliens Come From?

Aliens alluded to their place of origin in only a handful of cases. In one situation, aliens declared they "hailed from a planet called Clarion." Another group of aliens said they were "Psycheans." In sample two, one alien of a group said they were from a dying planet called "Janos." In two other cases, aliens said they were from other planets but would not identify them. Finally, some aliens said they "came from 2.4 million light-years away."[33]

How Did Aliens Travel Such Vast Distances across Space?

In the case where an alien claimed traveling 2.4 million light-years, this figure represented 14,160,000,000,000,000,000 miles. This is 14.2 quintillion miles! How could they come from such a distance? In another case, they said their ships "traveled via interdimensional portals." According to one alien, "a light ship traveled interdimensionally on light particles." This alien spoke of death, as well as the existence of many other dimensions. Could this alien's comment mark a link between the UFO phenomenon and the NDE?

Who Are Aliens? Do They Have Names?

An alien from Clarion said her name was Ciama. No other aliens in the sample identified themselves.

Why Did Aliens Come to Earth? What Was Their Purpose?

Aliens identified practical, global, and individual reasons for coming to Earth. One practical purpose, for instance, was "obtaining water." Also, they had global concerns—or, perhaps, universal/intergalactic concerns. They presented themselves as peace emissaries. They advised humans "to pray" and promised to return; one even specified returning "on October 7." Another alien said that his race "regularly transported humans to other planets to colonize them." When a planet was close to overpopulation, they started a war to reduce the population on that planet. He warned that Earth was in danger of breaking apart. Finally, some aliens came for individual reasons. For instance, one came "to take possession of a human's [witness's] soul."

Another arrived "to impregnate her [a witness]." In this case, a doctor confirmed the witness's pregnancy.

What Do Aliens Say about the Future of Earth?

Aliens have a dismal picture of Earth's future. In sample one, humans were admonished by aliens. This was done in 1950, 1971, 1977, and 1997. For instance, they said there were "places on Earth where there was too much power." A witness was shown "three-dimensional pictures of atomic explosions and some planet destroyed by too much power." In sample two, an alien said he wanted "to stop us from destroying the Earth." Aliens told witnesses dire events, including major catastrophes that would happen on Earth in the near future. Aliens also indicated that they would colonize Earth after humans destroyed themselves. They implored humans to take time to understand themselves, as time was drawing near when such understanding would be necessary.

These messages paralleled earthly events. As we all know, at the height of the Cold War (1950s-60s), the United States and Russia were archenemies. Each had thousands of nuclear missiles aimed at the other. Later, in the 1970s and onward, humans turned their attention to the physical environment.[34] Climate change became a major concern as droughts, hurricanes, and worldwide temperatures became increasingly threatening to the planet. Did aliens act as messengers of reconciliation, fostering peace and environmental harmony on Earth? Did humans project their fears onto the alien forms they saw before them?

Public Opinion about UFOs

What were Americans' views about UFOs? Table 2.11 summarizes recent American attitudes toward UFOs and ETs, including the ways in which humans may react to evidence about both.

Table 2.11: Public Opinion about UFOs and Aliens

Questions:	Respondents' Opinions:
	(Percent answering yes)
1. Read/heard about UFOs?	87% (Gallup, 1997)
2. Do UFOs exist?	65% (Sky News, 2002)
3. Have you or another seen UFOs?	6% (Life Magazine, 2000)
4. What are UFOs?	25% alien spacecraft 19% normal events misinterpreted (Roper, 1999)
5. Is there life beyond Earth?	80% (CIRM Institute-Italy, 2002)
6. Does extraterrestrial life have intelligence?	54% (CNN/Time, 1997)
7. Have aliens contacted humans?	64% (CNN, 1997)
8. Have aliens contacted the government?	37% (CNN/Time, 1997)
9. Has government revealed all it knows about UFOs?	72% not telling everything (SciFi/Roper, 2002)
10. Which professionals should make first contact?	29% scientists (Roper, 1999)
11. How prepared are you to learn there are ETs?	74% somewhat prepared (SciFi/Roper, 2002)
12. How would general population react to evidence ETs exist and visited Earth?	36% would be very concerned; 32% would be fully prepared to handle it (Roper, 1999)
13. How do aliens look?	39% very much like humans 35% somewhat like humans (CNN/Time, 1997)
14. How will aliens treat us?	44% as friends (CNN/Time, 1997)

15. Have aliens abducted humans?	50% yes (CNN/Time, 1997) but 20% yes (SciFi/Roper, 2002)
16. Have you or an acquaintance been abducted?	93% no (CNN/Time, 1997)

As table 2.11 showed,[35] at least four out of five Americans in 1997 had heard or read about UFOs. Five years later (in 2002), 65 percent believed they existed. Only 6 percent personally saw a UFO or knew someone who had. When asked what UFOs were, 25 percent of respondents thought they were alien spacecraft. Only 19 percent considered them normal events that were misunderstood as UFOs.

As many as 80 percent of respondents thought life existed beyond Earth. A slight majority (54 percent) said it was intelligent. Some 64 percent thought aliens contacted humans, and 37 percent thought they contacted the federal government. Three out of four people held the opinion that the government concealed its knowledge of UFOs.

A staggering 74 percent of respondents thought they were prepared to receive information about the existence of ETs. But only 32 percent of these people thought the general public was ready. Respondents thought scientists should be among the first to make contact with ETs. There was a general opinion that ETs looked similar to humans, and that they would treat humans as friends. Half (50 percent) of the respondents thought humans were abducted by aliens, while 90 percent said neither they nor an acquaintance had ever had such an experience.

The American mind is a fertile place for the alien story to take root: 80 percent of them believed there was life beyond Earth; 54 percent thought this life had intelligence; 50 percent believed aliens abducted humans; and 37 percent thought ETs contacted the federal government. Almost three out of four interviewees claimed they were prepared to receive information about ETs. Their fear of them was muted by the fact that they thought ETs looked like them. Also, respondents thought aliens would treat them as friends.

Some skepticism does persist. For instance, while the majority heard and believed in this phenomenon, 19 percent thought these objects were of human origin (e.g., mistaken as airplanes). Also, while the majority was prepared to receive information about ETs' existence, only 33 percent thought others were so inclined. While about one out of three thought ETs contacted the federal government, 72 percent thought the government concealed this knowledge. There is a story being created that is a mystery. The true nature of this phenomenon is neither totally known nor wholly believed.

3

UFO CASES

Chapter 2 presented basic information about UFOs, aliens, and human witnesses. This chapter offers an in-depth sociological description of four alien planets.

The source of data used to describe the social structure of alien worlds originated with four books written by Wendelle C. Stevens. He is the author of more than thirty books, and many depict life on other planets. Since his death in 2010 at the age of eighty-seven, Mr. Stevens's books have become collectibles. (This has driven their prices into the hundreds, and, in some cases, into the thousands of dollars. I was fortunate enough to purchase four of his texts before their rise in value in the late 1980s and early 1990s.) As stated, these books form the basis for a description of life on other worlds, as presented in this chapter. I purchased these four books because their titles suggested that they contained information about alien societies:[1]

1. *UFO Contact from Planet Acart: From Utopia to Reality*
2. *UFO Abduction at Botucatu: A Preliminary Report*
3. *UFO . . . Contact from Planet Iarga: A Report of the Investigation*
4. *UFO Contact from Planet Ummo: The Incredible Truth* (vol. 2)

This chapter is divided into sections, with one section for each of the four books. Within each of these sections, six sociological concepts (i.e., *demography, culture, stratification, institutions, social problems,* and *social change*) will serve as conceptual lenses that reveal the social structure of the four alien worlds. This format will allow us to compare and contrast these other worlds.

Book #1:
UFO Contact from Planet Acart: From Utopia to Reality

Incident Described

Artur Berlet drove a tractor for the municipality of Sarandi, Rio Grande do Sul, in Brazil. He was a part-time photographer, married with two children. He had a three-year-old daughter and one-year-old son. The book described this incident as one of the earliest abductions in modern times.

Artur "was gone for nine terrestrial days, from May 14 to 23, 1958."[2] He was walking to the city of Sarandi at about 7:00 a.m., and had just passed a farm (belonging to Dr. Dionisio Peretti). The witness then saw a strange light above some trees about two hundred meters (656 feet) away, and he came to within one hundred feet of it. He observed a rounded object, approximately one hundred feet in diameter, with a construction of what looked like two bowls inverted one on top of the other. The UFO had a red-to-ash-colored opaque light coming from it. Two shadows then appeared, and a strong beam of light hit the witness as he lost consciousness.

He reported going to another planet in a UFO, which was thirty meters (ninety-eight feet) in diameter, propelled by solar energy, and shaped like the one he saw over the trees. The trip took thirty hours and covered sixty-two million kilometers. The spacecraft traveled at four hundred to five hundred kilometers per second.[3]

When he awoke, he found himself in a "milky white" hospital bed on a craft. The room was rectangular with one rounded side. The aliens fastened his arms, loosened them, lifted him up, and took him to a nearby compartment. They gave him a long cape with sleeves extending to his feet.

After the craft had landed, they took him into a street where he saw buildings of various colors and types. The streets were six feet wide, with many pedestrians dressed in strange-colored jumpsuits and no vehicular traffic. Aircraft landed on tops of buildings.

Two beings escorted Artur into a tall, metal building with an interior of upholstery-like cloth. Exterior building walls emitted light that nearly blinded him. He was in a temporary prison with walls of a thick, furry fabric. Water gushed out of a pipe, and there was a small table and a bed. He lied down and felt hungry. Two males and a female entered his room and brought him food that looked like gelatin. They also gave him dark, grain-like bread and something like soup. The witness described some of this food as having a repugnant smell.

Another being with a smile on his face patted Artur on the back as if to say, "Calm down; everything is okay."[4] They then entered a five- to six-story building, where he undressed in a bathroom, showered, and dressed in trousers and a shirt. Previously, the aliens had treated the witness as a prisoner, but now they treated him as a guest.

Artur found himself in a room with a rectangular table and high-backed chairs. There were about fifteen others in the space. Soon, a heavyset, middle-aged male alien, with a juvenile smile entered and told Artur to "sit down." When Artur asked the alien's name, he replied, "Acorc Cat." The beings reassured Artur, and then they ate.

When finished, they each said good-bye by placing a hand on Artur's shoulder. Artur and the creatures boarded a vehicle, and then, with the touch of a lever, they ascended. Solar energy powered the vehicle. Although no vehicles drove on the ground, they filled the sky. Acorc took Artur to visit his family in their city, "Con." Their vehicle landed on a pad outside the family's apartment on the tenth floor. They went into a room furnished with a small table and a screen on the wall. Acorc Cat's wife was on the screen. Acorc called his friend, Tuec, on a phone, and, shortly afterward, Acorc's wife and daughter arrived.

The daughter had blue eyes and straw-colored hair that fell over her shoulders. She was tall, with an oval face, white skin, a medium-size mouth and lips, and a thin nose. She wore a dress that fell to her feet, with embroidery on the sleeves and bodice. She asked Artur if he had a large family, and if he was comfortable being on another planet. She peppered him with a host of other questions.

They then went in an elevator to a terrace that looked out over a "majestic and beautiful" city. (See chapter 4, "A Friendly Family," in *UFO Contact from Planet Acart*.) Acorc pointed out universities, factories, and government buildings. When Artur felt hungry, he asked how many meals a day they ate. Acorc replied, "Five." Acorc told Artur that he would meet the Son of the Sun, who was their governor. It was he who would determine if, and when, Artur could return to Earth. Acorc told Artur he had to be unconscious on his trip back for his own physical safety. They "dropped him off" about three miles from his city (Sarandi, Brazil). Artur was weak, but arrived home nine days after disappearing.

Planet's Environment

There were twenty billion inhabitants on Acart. It was not a blue planet, even though it had an ocean. It had four colors: one from the ground, another from the water, another from the corona around the globe of their planet, and another that came up almost as far as the space platform (thirty-one thousand miles from Acart). The weather on the planet was intensely cold, but there was a warm beach area. The beach had sand and a row of trees. The witness described it as a "veritable paradise."(See chapter 19, "Marine Recreation," in *UFO Contact from Planet Acart*.) This planet had only one season. The sky was almost the color of lead, and the sun was not as brilliant as Earth's. There were continents separated by seas, at least one river, and a mountainous region. There was no moon, but there were two gigantic, orbiting space platforms populated with thousands of beings and vehicles. Acart had some very large cities, and the capital was Con, where Acorc and his family lived.

Demography: Aliens' Characteristics

Acartians looked much like humans, but paler. As a race, they were white with straw-colored or dark hair. They had a medium stature, but were greater in size than humans. Their blood was blue, not red.

The witness reported about individual Acartians, not the beings as a group. For instance, the wife of the Son of the Sun was tall and a little heavy, with straw-colored hair. Her skin was deathly pallid and ashened. Her mouth was not too big, but she had full, slightly protruding lips. She had a fine semilong nose, and bright, large, active eyes. This creature examined all who passed by. She had an independent personality.

The son of the Son of the Sun was ten years old, and had the same personality and similar looks as his mother. The daughter was sixteen or seventeen years old. She was slender, tall, and "Flat as a board, without any curves. Her neck was long and slender." Artur was afraid of her "Pointed chin, gash of a mouth, long teeth, and narrow and long nose. Her eyes were more oval, like Cleopatra's, and her hair was long and loose with little color to it." (See chapter 11, "A Lunch with the Son of the Sun," in *UFO Contact from Planet Acart*.)

Purpose/Message

The Acartians had three reasons for contacting humans. They wanted to: (1) learn about humans; (2) instruct earthlings in the use of solar energy, persuading them to give up atomic energy; and (3) explore Earth, which Acartians wanted to occupy after humans killed themselves in a nuclear war.

They abducted Artur for bread! They told Artur they wanted him to teach them how to grow grain for bread. Their bread grew on trees, and it did not taste too good to them. They wanted to learn how to plant wheat.

Culture

Nonmaterial Components of Culture

Acartian years, months, days, and hours translated into the following formula:

1 year   = 353 days (but, every 6 years, they drop 1 day = 352 days)
11 months = 1 year
32 days   = 1 month (the first month has 33 days except in the 6th year that has 32 days)
46 hours   = 1 day (Acartian hours are divided into 1/10ths and 1/100ths)
(Inconsistency with the numbers cited [e.g., 32 days x 11 months = 352 days, and not 353 days] is due to a discrepancy in the original text.)

In Earth terms, Acartian time translated into the following (according to Berlet's calculations):

1 Acartian year = 675 Earth days (1.8 Earth years)
1 Acartian month = 61 days and 8 hours Earth time
1 Acartian hour = 7 hours and 40 minutes Earth time

Artur forgot the names of the meals, but he felt that Acartians "ate all day"; he also said that they never ate a meal without saying a prayer. Acartians consumed alcoholic beverages in their homes, but not in public places. Such drink was made from fruit. They went to bed at four-tenths of the first hour of the night.

Values

The following values formed the foundation of the Acartian society:

> *Work*—an Acartian value, evident from the fact that all Acartians were eager to work. The impression

was that Acartians had a Marxian viewpoint. They distinguished between work and labor. The first was desirable, and the second was drudgery.

Noninterference—another Acartian value, and a principle that guided their relations with those from other planets. They felt compelled by their religious and moral beliefs neither to interfere with the internal workings of other planets nor to invade them.

Competition and *Recreation*—two other Acartian values, as witnessed by the sports they played. (Apparently, these two values were extremely important, as they commanded the longest chapter in *UFO Contact from Planet Acart* [chapter 25]; or, perhaps, this simply reflected the values of the book's author.)

Equality—another Acartian value, deduced from the fact that they did not have a system of stratification. Such a system would recognize inequality among individuals, so the lack of one would effectively indicate that they valued equality. In fact, their governor (the Son of the Sun) was an equal among Acartian citizens. He neither lived in a better house nor sat in a plush area at public events (e.g., sporting events).

Compassion and *Peace*—two other Acartian values. Acartians saw that God created all, and there was no need to accumulate riches or to preach falsehoods, intrigue, or disunity. Everyone should be united. Beings should give freely to each other the things God bestowed upon them.

Knowledge—another important Acartian value, as Acartians sought to learn about everything.

Efficiency—another Acartian value, and one that guided Acartians on their (and any other) overpopulated planet. They had to be efficient, or they could not meet the needs of so many beings.

Status and Role

Acartian males studied until they were eleven years old, and then they worked in professions approved by their schools. They worked until they were thirty-six years old, and then they retired. Females also studied until they were eleven years old. After this time, they either married and cared for the home, or they worked in various professions. The role of females in the home was similar to that of human women prior to feminism. For example, Acorc's wife always made the meals without Acorc's assistance, and it was she who always accompanied their children.

Daily Routine, Social Etiquette/Ceremonies and Rituals

Acartians greeted and left each other by placing their hands on one another's shoulders. If they knew each other well, they extended both hands, one on each shoulder. If they knew someone slightly, only one hand was placed on the other's shoulder. They did not shake each other's hands.

Students congregated to take part in parades and celebrations for the Son of the Sun. These events took place the night before "Guard Day." (The purpose of this was not disclosed.) A young Acartian brought a blank piece of paper to a sporting event, and gave it to the Son of the Sun, who waved it in the air, after which symbols appeared on the paper.

Material Components of Culture

Housing

Houses were much like they are on Earth, but with one important exception: they had platforms attached where their airplanes landed. They needed these platforms because airplanes were their mode of transportation. Houses no higher than one hundred feet, prefabricated, and composed of laminated steel. Lights emanated two to three meters outward from the walls of houses, although there were no streetlights.

Transportation

Acartians had streets, but they did not use them for motorized transport. As the roads were only six feet wide, Acartians used them for pedestrian traffic only. There were no cars on the planet. Acartians traveled in aircraft. Because transportation occurred in the sky (other than pedestrians walking on the roads), Acartian traffic problems were in the air and not on the ground. There was also some underground transportation in tunnels, air travel predominated.

Interplanet travel occurred on disc-shaped craft. These spaceships had furniture that came out of the walls. The ship that took Artur home had three levels. The bottom level had small ships, weapons, and such; the second level, which was in the middle, had dorms, storage spaces, labs, rooms, and corridors. The top level had control, locomotion, and defense systems. The ship moved by means of motors that used solar energy in conjunction with the magnetic push-pull of objects. This is the same force that moves planets, and, in fact, the attraction and repulsion of forces from each planet and its respective sun generated the power to move the ship through space. (The neutral zone was the area where there was no such push-pull.) (See chapter 27, "Return Voyage," in UFO from Planet Acart.) Thirty individuals controlled the craft. Acorc said they had ships floating around Earth, but not landing on it.

Technology

Flying discs were thirty to thirty-five meters (98 to 115 feet) in diameter and constructed from molds. There were ten solar motors that propelled a ship in the Acartian atmosphere. As described above, these spaceships moved by magnetic waves emitted from planets. The motor produced a vibration that created a magnetic wave, just like the ones emitted by planets; thus, one blocked, while the other attracted. When something on each side of the craft retracted, it controlled aircraft speed.

Social Stratification

Acartians had no social classes. The head of government, the Son of the Sun, did not have a higher status, because Acart lacked a system of social stratification. The Son of the Sun did not live in a mansion, and he "had the same rights and responsibilities as everyone else." The Acartians selected him "[A]s one among them who would guide their destinies. Once they selected him, the Son [sic] transformed their desires into laws and their words into orders. This leader, however, could not accrue power to benefit themselves [sic] but only to have laws made for the common good." (See chapter 11, "A Lunch with the Son of the Sun," in *UFO Contact from Planet Acart*.)

Social Institutions

Family

Acorc Cat's family was the only family described in the book. Assuming this family lived in a normative fashion, I inferred that Acartian marriages were monogamous, as this marriage consisted of only one male and one female. Also, they seemed to have nuclear families comprised of a husband, wife, and children. For instance, the Son of the Sun's family consisted of a wife, son, and daughter.

Religion

Acartians were *theists* because they believed in God and recognized him as creator of Earth, Acart, and all beings. They believed God created them for good. They believed God would "not give them things, but will delegate a man of some intelligence and worth to give the necessary knowledge." (See chapter 9, "A City at Night," in *UFO Contact from Planet Acart*.)

As stated previously, Acartians said prayers before meals. These prayers took place in the home but not in public places; not because they were private in their devotion, but because they were practical. It was too noisy in public places to pray.

Economy

Money did not exist on the planet. (See chapter 7, "Going to a Restaurant," in *UFO Contact from Planet Acart*.) Artur discovered this fact when he and Acorc were at a restaurant. He wanted to pay for drinks, but when he reached into his pocket to get some money, he realized that all he had was Brazilian money. He then learned that they did not use money on Acart. How did their economy work without the exchange of money? Acartians took whatever they wanted or needed, but nothing more. The old did not have to work, but Acartians of all ages did work because they wished to do so. Every year, they took the time to travel. Males worked until they were thirty years old, and then they retired. Females often were homemakers, but some worked outside the home; and those who did fell under the same system as working males.

At one time in Acartian history, there were many countries with their own monetary systems. This system yielded a very rich minority (10 percent), while the majority (90 percent) was very poor. This stratification of individuals led to many crimes committed by the poor because they were miserable. A scientist then invented a machine that harnessed the power of the sun for energy production, and this energy could be used as a weapon. He demonstrated its power, and then he demanded all countries to unite into one, and to abandon the use of money and the pursuit of profit. All agreed, and they asked him to govern the new, unified Acart. They called him the "Man of the Sun." He refused the governorship, but offered his son in his place. His son took the position, taking the title of the "Son of the Sun." (See chapter 20, "A Planet without Money," in *UFO Contact from Planet Acart*.)

Acartians had farms and factories. They did not plow their fields, which produce little due to erosion. Instead, Acartians used stepped terraces for farming. They used tractors similar to ours, but their engines made no noise because they used solar power. Animals, such as buffalo with one horn, were like cattle, providing food, hides (used for fabric), and milk.

Factories were in mountainous regions because these places were inhospitable for farming, and because the biggest mines for producing solar steel were located there. Artur went to a factory that was ten kilometers (6.2 miles) long, five hundred meters (approximately 1,640 feet) wide, and thirty meters (98 feet) high. The roof was one sheet of metal that served as a landing field for airplanes. There were three lines of columns, and one crossing in the middle. Conceivably, it would take one and a half hours to cross the factory on foot.

Both machines and Acartians fashioned metal into different products, such as electric lamps, TVs, and weapons. These weapons, however, did not shoot bullets or other ammunition; rather, they emitted a strong light powered by solar energy. Each weapon shot out two hundred volts, which could kill an Acartian. More powerful weapons were for spacecraft, and they could destroy a building at two to three kilometers (about one and a half miles). Another weapon, called a "neutralizer," could destroy an object up to five thousand kilometers (over 3,100 miles) away. This weapon could destroy human life but leave buildings intact. Different products (e.g., the skeleton of a solar ship and solar ship motors) were manufactured in different sections of the factory. This indicated they utilized *specialization* as an organizing principle.

Government

As previously mentioned, the capital of Acart was the city of Con. (See chapter 26, "Good-byes," in *UFO Contact from Planet Acart*.) There was not much information about their governmental structure, but Artur noted that "if you took a little from all the governments on Earth, you'd have theirs." (See questionnaire section in *UFO Contact from Planet Acart*.) The government building was round. The room Artur and the creatures were in was rounded on three sides and flat on the fourth. The rounded part held many desks with chairs. The desks were one behind the other in lines, rising in stepped levels. There was a six-meter-long row with nine or ten shoulder-high chairs near the flat wall.

Again, the Son of the Sun was the head of the government, but he did not receive any payment or recognition that placed him above anyone else. Consequently, he sat in the middle and presided over a meeting of about five hundred council members. They deliberated on the question of permitting Artur's return to Earth. Some council members thought Artur might bring news about their planet back to humans, who in turn might threaten Acart. (See chapter 10, "Their Government Decides," in *UFO Contact from Planet Acart*.) The Son of the Sun decided that because Artur had come to Acart unwillingly, he should be returned to Earth.

As previously stated, there were no countries on Acart. The inhabitants had abolished them through mutual consent, about a hundred years after their wars ended. The entire planet constituted their country. No social stratification existed, and everyone was equal. The inhabitants of Acart were the government. They had elections that were somewhat like Earth's democracies. (See chapter 8, "Homesick and Alarmed at the End of the Day," in *UFO Contact from Planet Acart*.) The Acartians picked a governor (currently, the Son of the Sun) every three years.

Recreation

Acorc took Artur to a "recreation city" near the Acartian seacoast. (See chapter 19, "Marine Recreation," in *UFO Contact from Planet Acart*.) While they traveled there, they passed over several cities. As they approached the recreational city, they passed over a building that was some twenty kilometers (slightly over twelve miles) in length. This building, which curved with the shape of the beach, had two floors. The first floor had juice bars, eateries, and changing rooms; the second floor had dormitories.

Artur described two sports played on Acart. (See chapter 25, "A Sports Field," in *UFO Contact from Planet Acart*.) The first sport was played on a field no longer than a basketball court. The field of artificial grass measured eighty by one hundred meters (98 by 328 feet). Balconies and a gallery surrounded the field. Artur and the Son of the Sun sat in the gallery area, but the bleachers and galleries were described equally as "comfortable." The stadium had a removable roof powered by solar energy. When a bell rang, everyone stood as the Son of the Sun, his family, and a few others entered the stadium.

There was a white line across the middle of the field. It extended twenty meters (sixty-five feet, six inches). The Acartians then drew another line ten meters back from the first line. Another line twenty meters long connected the first two lines. Twenty males, ten on each side, faced one another across the middle line. Two of them pushed each other backward, and each tried to get the other past the line behind the midfield line. The team with the most members pushed behind this line won.

Uniforms identified the teams. One team wore dark, knee-length pants, and the other wore light ones. All of them wore parachutist-type boots with cleats, and shirts with insignias.

Each team's members were equally matched. This game ended with the score 6 to 4. The Son of the Sun gave medallions to the winning team. Also, the first player who pushed his opponent past the white line received a larger medallion.

The second game had two goals placed at opposite ends of the field, for a distance of one hundred meters (328 feet). There were three smaller goals between them.

Teams consisted of thirteen members each, and squad members wore light and dark pants. Four more males were present as "arbitrators" who coordinated and directed the game. They seemed to play with a soccer-like ball, which they kicked.

Scoring occurred when someone kicked the ball around the goal, not into it. If the ball went around a smaller goal, the team got one-fifth of a point. If it went around a large goal, the team received two-fifths of a point. If the ball circumvented a large goal two consecutive times, the team earned 2.5 fifths each time. The winning team scored 10 four-fifths points, while the losers scored 10 one-fifth points.

Social Problems

Overpopulation

With ninety million beings living in an Acartian city, it was not hard to imagine the predominant social problem on their planet was overpopulation. In fact, because of this social problem, Acartians came to Earth. They did not plan to invade Earth. They merely planned to colonize it, after humans killed themselves in a worldwide nuclear war.

War

There was no war on Acart, although there had been a nuclear one. They had two weapons: a solar disintegrator and a solar neutralizer. They used the first in war, and the second in medicine and farming. They had gone through their own nuclear age, and they had developed technology (i.e., solar neutralizer) to deal with radiation. The solar neutralizer would be used to cleanse Earth from radiation caused by nuclear war. Acartians would then repopulate the Earth. They had their own weapons, but they were not guns. They were more like flashlights that hung from the belt of those in positions of authority.

Poverty

As mentioned, this social problem once existed on Acart, at the time when they had a stratified society with the rich on top and the poor on lower levels. The pursuit of profit created a poorer class. When they abandoned stratification, poverty ended. Now everyone pursued what he or she wanted and needed. All desired to do the necessary work to keep such a system afloat.

Crime

During the time when they had countries with rich and poor (i.e., when they were socially stratified), Acartians had crime, which they acknowledged.[5] The poor committed crimes but were not placed in jail. They worked just like everyone else, but were denied the rights of other Acartians. These individuals could not go into public places or travel to other cities.

Social Change

Acart went through two major social changes. First, they shifted from nation-states to a universal, planetary government. They did this after they nearly annihilated themselves in a nuclear war. As described, a scientist, the so-called Man of the Sun, developed technology that controlled their sun's energy. Acartians conceded to the Man of the Sun's demand to unite into one planetary society. They did this when they saw they could be destroyed.

The second social change concerned *stratification*. Again, as previously stated, there had been rich and poor strata on Acart, but this led to a population distribution where 90 percent were poor and 10 percent were rich. The extent of this inequality led to an increased rate of crime, which threatened their society. Thus, Acartians decided to abandon stratification, and, with it, the pursuit of profit. Now everyone worked, and each received whatever they wanted and needed, but not to excess. Knowing how well their system functioned provided them with an incentive to continue.

Conclusion

Acartian society was surely Gesellschaft in social organization, which is because of its high degree of organization and complexity. For instance, their governmental structure evolved from a nation–state model to a universal, planetary form. Their technology was complex. For example, they developed transportation systems that enabled them to visit distant planets (e.g., Earth). They harnessed solar energy for farming and medicine, as well as for weaponry. Moreover, they also had a complicated system for daily air travel, more complex than any road system we have on Earth. Additionally, they had a retractable roof on their sports stadium, artificial grass in their sports complex, TV screens on walls for telephone calls (e.g., the one on which Acorc saw his wife), and cell-like telephones (e.g., the one on which Acorc called his friend, Tuec).[6] They did seem to have traditional social forms (by earthly standards), despite their sophisticated technology. Although females worked outside of the home, their behaviors at home seemed traditional. They made meals and raised children without the help of male spouses, for instance.

The Acartian society seemed to be socialistic, rather than capitalistic, for it focused on the common good, not on individual self-interest. For instance, they had no money for buying and selling. If they needed or wanted something, they simply went to a factory and got it. No one took anything in excess.

The Acartian diagram-for-social-living underwent a huge social change as it dealt with three enormous problems-in-social-living: (1) the pursuit of profit produced an imbalance in wealth, and this inequality fostered an increase in their crime rate as the poor dealt with their misery; (2) they had a large overpopulation problem; and (3) they barely survived a planetary nuclear war.

Where 10 percent of the Acartian population had been rich, 90 percent had been poor. This imbalance created a latent function of developing a large increase in their crime rates. Acartians decided to eliminate stratification in order to deal with this social problem. Consequently, everyone resided on the same social strata and possessed the same standard of living. (For example, when the Son of the Sun showed up at the sports stadium, he and his entourage sat in the same seats as every other spectator.) Thus, they moved from a system of stratification to an equalitarian society. Inequality, or discrimination, gave way to equality as a social value.

Second, their global population exploded. This social problem had the latent function of driving their space program. They explored distant planets in the hope of finding habitable places to resettle their burgeoning population.

Third, their nuclear war inspired a scientist (the Man of the Sun) to invent technology that eliminated future nuclear wars. The solar neutralizer and solar disintegrator persuaded leaders of Acartian countries to abandon their nation-states for a universal planetary government. As members of the same society, war became obsolete.

Finally, the portrait of planet Acart as described by Artur Berlet and Wendelle C. Stevens demonstrated a place where technological advancement soared ahead of social development. Spacecraft traveled millions of miles, landed on Earth, and were not detected due to its stealth technology. This technology, however, was far ahead of their husband-and-wife marital roles and their monogamous marriage form. Perhaps Acartians, like humans, experience culture lag; that is, their technology moved ahead of their social arrangements. In fact, the social organization of their marriages and families appear to be more like *Ozzie and Harriet* of the 1950s than the futuristic *Star Trek*. Acorc went to work, and his wife stayed home with their children.

Book #2
UFO Abduction at Botucatu: A Preliminary Report

Incident Described

Joao Valerio had more than twenty contacts and five abductions with ETs, but his first episode happened in 1982.[7] Joao worked[8] at Santa Casa de Misericordia, a public hospital in Botucatu, Sao Paulo, Brazil. His friends described him as stable, a hard worker, and a good man who neither smoked nor drank.[9]

It was nighttime and very dark. Joao went outside to a backyard water tank for water to take his medicine. Suddenly, behind him there was a beam of light with a being inside of it. The light functioned as an elevator, and drew Joao and the being upward into a room. Another being took them into a second room containing two more beings. These two beings were talking with one another, and motioned to Joao to sit on a circular chair. They left by walking through a wall!

From behind him, a dark-skinned, human-looking, brunette walked through another wall. She was naked! Initially, Joao thought he was in heaven among angels, but when he saw the naked female, he did not think so. She approached him and put her hand close to his face. He fainted. They then took him to another room where they laid him down, and attached two apparatuses to him: one to his chest, and the other on his penis. Two males helped the female mount Joao. The female and Joao then had sex!

Joao woke up at five the next morning. His wife and daughter found him in their backyard. He was naked and had an oily substance all over him. There were marks on his throat and the right side of his chest, and he was dazed. His wife and daughter brought him inside. They gave him a bath. He woke up from his shock about an hour later, and went to the police station to report the incident. A doctor examined him, but could not explain the marks on his chest and thorax. Joao explained that the marks on his throat were the result of the beam of light that had hit him, drawing him into a spacecraft.

About three months later, on March 6, 1983, an alien abducted Joao. A being named RAMA appeared beneath the window, and Joao flew outside and met him. The witness said he flew over houses and fields, and that he communicated with RAMA via telepathy. Later, when he returned home, although it was pouring, Joao was bone-dry. He had a blue stone that smelled like the liquid the ETs put on him.

After another one of his trips, when he returned home, Joao was floating, with a luminescent body and two beams of light coming out of his eyes. People noticed a neck chain before he was abducted. Joao had locked it, but it flew off him. At one point, the chain was on the floor of his house, and it spelled the letter R backward. At another time, the neck chain was in a backyard tree, in the form of an upside-down triangle. (See chapter 7, "The Diary," in *Abduction at Botucatu: A Preliminary Report.*)

Planet's Environment

Although Joao went on numerous trips (by his accounting, twenty of them, but his friends counted forty-two), there was scant description of the places he visited. On his first trip, he described an "arid, desert-like place with sand and rocks." On two other trips, he described a place with "small trees, like on Earth."

Joao did not know the name of the planet he visited, but said it was behind Earth's moon. He described their days and nights as being very short. He said he saw three nights in an eighteen-hour period of Earth time. (See chapter 6, "The Interview," in *UFO Abduction at Botucatu: A Preliminary Report.*) He said their atmosphere was very clean, soft, and pure. He did not see a sun in their sky, and explained that their light emanated from the walls of houses.

Demography: Aliens' Characteristics

The female Joao encountered on the UFO had black eyes shaped like those of the Japanese. Her naked body revealed medium-sized breasts and pubic hair. She had curved eyebrows like human women, but most of these alien females had eyebrows that were straighter and longer. Aliens on the first planet Joao experienced were all the same height (five feet, nine inches tall); they had black hair, light complexions, and faces with almost the same features. He described them as looking like humans and being strong. Joao said the beings looked gentle and had nice skin.

The first time RAMA was on Earth, he wore a cloth mask and a hood with holes for his eyes. ETs used masks that covered their faces and wore hoods on their heads when they were in contact with humans. They removed these when they were on their own planet.

Purpose/Message

The messages RAMA gave to Joao had to deal with macro and micro levels of social living. On the macro level, RAMA talked about the condition of planet Earth; on the micro level, he gave Joao personal advice.

In the first part of the book, the ETs told a Swiss farmer that humans were in ecological danger. To avoid this danger, humans had to change Earth's "mass mind." (See introduction, in *UFO Abduction at Botucatu: A Preliminary Report.*) The aliens recommended a grassroots effort. They said no one would come to save Earth because (1) we made our own mess; and (2) helping us would result in their interfering in our evolutionary learning process, which would stunt our growth.

They said Earth's destruction would take place in "1980–something." There would be fires and earthquakes and strong winds that would destroy everything. Also, they told Joao that the old countries (i.e., Asia and Europe) would be destroyed in a war starting in 1985. (See chapter 6, "The Interview," in *UFO Abduction at Botucatu: A Preliminary Report.*) The younger countries would be protected (it was unknown who or what would provide such protection). The aliens forecasted these catastrophes: falling buildings and trees, big floods and strong winds, and humans fleeing in fear. Joao said aliens wanted to help humans. What humans must do was to believe in aliens, and then earthlings would be saved. Future occurrences would occur, and they could not change. The message appeared in an alien language, so humans would believe they existed. (The alien message had a strong resemblance to the Protestant doctrine of "believe and be saved.")

Aliens went to Brazil because they thought that Brazil (1) was a very tolerant country; (2) had no racial barriers; (3) had a long history of peaceful coexistence; (4) had proper humility, and respect for other nations and for individuals; and (5) did not seek to dominate countries or to control individuals.

On the micro-level, RAMA informed Joao that he should stay in touch with the aliens because this group was "well mentalized, with much faith." (See chapter 7, "The Diary," in *UFO Abduction at Botucatu: A Preliminary Report.*) RAMA further told Joao, "to confirm that I am here, I will give you a signal." (See chapter 7, "The Diary," in *Abduction at Botucatu: A Preliminary Report.*) Shortly afterward, Joao saw a flash of light.

Culture

Nonmaterial Components of Culture

Language

When aliens talked, they moved their lips and made a sound like pigeons cooing. They also had a writing system. For instance, RAMA left a note for Joao, other aliens wrote on Joao's chest, and a beam of light that hit Joao's throat left a "table of hieroglyphics" on it, according to the inspector at the police station. (See chapter 1, "UFO Abduction at Botucatu," in *UFO Abduction at Botucatu: A Preliminary Report.*)

Norms

Later, RAMA told Joao, "Do not be afraid of your teachers. Why not keep my words. Do not think of tomorrow. Do not keep with you people who do not believe and [who] abuse you. You know who[m] I am speaking of. Have faith in your teachers and in ours!" (See chapter 7, "The Diary," in *UFO Abduction at Botucatu: A Preliminary Report.*)

On another occasion, RAMA said to Joao, "You will have to be prepared because it is close when you will go with us. Try to be charged, and don't wear yourself out." (See chapter 7, "The Diary," in *UFO Abduction at Botucatu: A Preliminary Report.*)

These instructions served to guide Joao toward his alien brothers and away from the earthly realm.

Values

The following values formed the bedrock of society on the alien planet:

> *Activity* and *Work*—Joao described the alien visitors as always walking and doing something. Apparently, they valued activity and work.

> *The Environment*—a major reason why aliens contacted humans was to warn people about their degradation of the environment. RAMA notified Joao that humans needed to alter their thinking about, and their use of, our earthly environment.

> *Self-Reliance*—*RAMA* offered humans his help, but also informed humanity that no one can do it for them. They made the mess, and it was up to them to take care of it. His culture did not permit dependence; it valued independence of action.

Material Components of Culture

Housing

Joao said these aliens lived in stone houses without doors. These stones had various colors, and he described them as very beautiful. From a distance, the stones looked yellow-gold, but as he got closer, they changed to white. When very close to them, they were gray. He thought these dwellings were more like caves than houses. The housing was isolated, not grouped together as occurs in cities.

Technology

When Joao saw "strange machines," he thought they were for warfare. He doubted his conclusion, though, because he did not see any weaponry on the planet.

Spacecraft

Joao described the alien spacecraft as five hundred meters (1,640 feet) long and disc-shaped. It was flat on the bottom and had a wide but low dome on top. A light beam extended from its bottom. As previously described, this beam functioned as an elevator to transport Joao and the aliens up and down from the craft to the ground. The UFO was orange, green, and lilac in color. In another section of the book, Joao described a UFO looking like a bell with a large part like a skirt, and having a smaller ring-type structure around it. He described the craft as approximately two stories high, but the interior ceilings were human-height. He left the craft from the lower level. When he was inside the UFO, he did not hear any noise, but when he was outside of it, the craft sounded like a swarm of bees or a loud transformer.

Artifacts

Stones

After Joao returned home, he found a blue stone in his bed. It smelled like the disinfectant liquid they had rubbed on him before he had sex with the alien female. In another instance, Joao felt something like an electrical shock in his right arm. A fork he held turned on its own, and bent. Also, there seemed to be healing power to this stone. A human woman with breast cancer did not get cancer in her other breast after meeting Joao.

Joao's wife broke the stone to observe what was inside of it. A red liquid poured out, and dried instantaneously. It "smelled like old kitchen grease or vitamins." (See chapter 6, "The Interview," in *UFO*

Abduction at Botucatu: A Preliminary Report.) She washed it, and the red liquid disappeared, leaving a square piece three inches long by two inches wide by one inch thick. A red triangle made of red veins was inside. In another section of the book, however, this stone had an oval shape, weighed five pounds, and had two coatings: a white substance on top, and a brown one on the bottom.

When Joao was eight years old, RAMA gave him another stone the size of a button. It moved on its own, and it once flew out of Joao's pocket. "It went up and down like a spider on a thread." (See chapter 6, "The Interview," in *UFO Abduction at Botucatu: A Preliminary Report.*) Evidently, he owned the stone for years, as it came out of his pocket and fell near his wife, but no one saw it again.

Photos

The ETs let Joao take nine pictures of their planet. The pictures were never visible on Earth.

[AUTHOR'S NOTE: *UFO Abduction at Botucatu: A Preliminary Report* did not include the following items: social stratification, social institutions, social problems, and social change.]

Conclusion

Joao described seeing lights and beings in the sky. At one time, with the influence of the Catholic Church in South America, people gave a religious interpretation to events like these. They thought these events were miracles and apparitions. As the UFO story took hold in Brazil and other South American countries, people viewed them as aliens and UFOs. Paranormal events took on a new, secularized interpretation.

In a like manner, norms that RAMA gave to Joao "to fear not" and "to believe in his sky-teachers" had a vague familiarity to them. It was terribly close to Christ's message to the apostles and his followers. That is, "Be faithful, and do not listen to false gods. Prepare yourself, for your life is with me in heaven." Has the author of *UFO Abduction at Botucatu: A Preliminary Report* taken the rich Christ story held by the dominant Catholic Church of South America, and secularized it by using its theme in the UFO genre? For instance, RAMA is an alien who came down to Earth to spread the word and save the planet from ecological devastation. Christ came down to Earth to spread the word of God and to save humanity from its sinful ways. Also, Mary Magdalene washed Christ's feet, while aliens cleansed Joao with a liquid disinfectant. Is there any correspondence here?

Another sociological understanding is to perceive the UFO story alongside of the Christ story within the context of social change. The Christ story was dominant in South American countries like Brazil. This happened during a time when the rural environment shaped their societies. Populations were small, and they lived in tribes spread throughout jungles and small villages. Their technology was simple, and their relationships were personal. In other words, their social organization was Gemeinschaft. As their social organization shifted to Gesellschaft, with a larger population and more complex technology, their stories changed.

For instance, lights in the sky, which people once thought was Christ enshrouded in light, became aliens entering the Earth's atmosphere on technologically advanced craft. The themes of these stories, however, remained the same. Christ and aliens came to Earth for the purpose of redemption. Christ came to save humanity from its sinful ways, while aliens arrived to save earthlings from wars and ecological disaster. The virtue of holiness and the wickedness of sin gave way to the secular transgressions of humanity against one another in war, and the degradation of their earthly place.

Book #3
UFO . . . Contact from Planet IARGA:
A Report of the Investigation

[AUTHORS' NOTE: The numbers in parentheses found below refer to pages in *UFO ... Contact from Planet Iarga.*]

Incident Described

Stefan Denaerde (pseudonym) and his wife, son, and small daughters were sailing on their yacht (*Tjalk*), six miles off the coast of the Netherlands in Oosterscheldt. Denaerde wrote, "Suddenly, out of the darkness, a strong, blue-white searchlight shone in my eyes from a point directly in front of the bow . . . and I heard a high-pitched whining noise above the noise of my motor." (See chapter 1, "Confrontation," in *UFO . . . Contact from Planet Iarga: A Report of the Investigation.* 14) "Then his boat came to a standstill against something solid . . . a flat thing in the water." (See chapter 1, "Confrontation," in *UFO . . . Contact from Planet Iarga: A Report of the Investigation.* 14)

He called out to see if anyone was there. The searchlight went on again. He then saw what he thought was a dead body in the water, and he jumped in to help. As he did so, much to his surprise, he landed on something, even though he was standing in only three feet of water!

The body had on "a metallic suit" and there was a "rubbery ball around its head." (See chapter 1, "Confrontation," in *UFO . . . Contact from Planet Iarga: A Report of the Investigation.* 15) Stefan said that "the rubbery ball reflected the blue light so much, I couldn't see the man's face." (See chapter 1, "Confrontation," in *UFO . . . Contact from Planet Iarga: A Report of the Investigation.* 15) He described a lot of diffused light under the water, and another being like the first one. This being was not dead. It approached him at a rapid pace. Stefan soon realized that the figure was not human! It had an animal-like face, with large, square pupils in the eyes. He described the being's eyes as "hypnotic" and "self-assured." (See chapter 1, "Confrontation," in *UFO . . . Contact from Planet Iarga: A Report of the Investigation.* 15)

The object in the water was about fifty feet in diameter, and it rested on a ledge. Initially, Stefan thought it was a magnet because the compasses on his yacht stopped working. A lid on top of the object opened, and two beings in spacesuits ascended in a herky-jerky motion. They carried some objects joined by cables or wires. They bowed toward him in a respectful manner, as if in greeting him.

The next morning, against his wife's wishes, Stefan went back to the spacecraft. The door slowly opened, and he looked down about eight feet, through an opening, which was about three feet wide. He saw a cube-shaped space about eight feet across, (See chapter 2, "Aboard the Alien Spacecraft," in *UFO . . . Contact from Planet Iarga: A Report of the Investigation.* 25) and he heard a voice say, "Welcome aboard." He went below.

Upon the craft, Stefan saw huge reels and drums that had cable and pipe wrapped around them. He saw what he thought was a desk with a normal-looking chair made of a metal frame and leather upholstery. There was a large screen (five feet wide by three feet high) that had a soft, green fluorescent glow.

Planet's Environment

Iarga, found in another solar system, was about ten light-years (58.7 trillion miles) from Earth. (See chapter 2, "Aboard the Alien Spacecraft," in *UFO . . . Contact from Planet Iarga: A Report of the Investigation.* 34) It had three g's of gravity, seven-bar atmospheric pressure, and high levels of nitrogen and ammonia. All these were greater than those on Earth. (See chapter 2, "Aboard the Alien Spacecraft," in *UFO . . . Contact from Planet Iarga: A Report of the Investigation.* 30) Iarga was a pink-white ball with two gigantic, flat, concentric rings that formed a halo around the planet. One was a small inner ring, and the other was a broad outer ring. These rings cast a sharp band on the clouds below. Iarga's rotation was slower than Earth's, thus making the days and nights longer than on Earth.

Iarga had a thick atmosphere, a layer of mist, and high air pressure. These factors created an environment of dim sunlight, and an inability to see the moon or stars. They called Earth a "blue planet with blinding light," while their planet was "green with misty light." (See chapter 2, "Aboard the Alien Spacecraft," in *UFO . . . Contact from Planet Iarga: A Report of the Investigation.* 35)

Iargan wind speeds could reach three times Earth's maximum wind speeds, and Iarga had a denser atmosphere than Earth's. Rains on Iarga were heavier than on Earth; in fact, the rains were so heavy, they could kill an unprotected human, and their snowfalls could be ten times greater than on Earth. Additionally, their earthquakes were more severe than Earth's. (See chapter 2, "Aboard the Alien Spacecraft," in *UFO . . . Contact from Planet Iarga: A Report of the Investigation.* 35)

They showed Stefan a holograph picture of the planet. From space, it looked pink, but from under its atmosphere, it was a mixture of yellow-gray, brown, and greenish clouds. These colors gave a very somber and threatening impression. Their ocean appeared bright green with white crests of waves. Stefan saw a white beach and horseshoe-shaped island. He also saw a bridge that stretched across the ocean.

The landscape was varied. (See chapter 2, "Aboard the Alien Spacecraft," in *UFO . . . Contact from Planet Iarga: A Report of the Investigation.* 36) It included green prehistoric forests, agriculture near buildings, and lakes between mountains. A deep ocean covered almost the entire planet, and its landmass consisted of several islands. The land was about the size of Australia. (See chapter 2, "Aboard the Alien Spacecraft," in *UFO . . . Contact from Planet Iarga: A Report of the Investigation.* 39) This configuration, coupled with their large population, created many social and planning problems.

Demography: Aliens' Characteristics

Iargans were humanoid in appearance, but did not look completely like humans. As previously described, their faces were animal-like in appearance. They had teeth and large eyes[10] with square pupils. Their heads were similar in size to humans, but their depth was greater. Their heads had a bony ridge in the middle of their skulls. This ridge switched into a deep groove in the center of their foreheads. Stefan thought their heads had two separate compartments. Their necks looked thicker than those of humans. Their arms and shoulders had the same proportion as humans, but were muscular and heavier. They possessed broad chests, short, stocky legs, and short-cropped hair on the top of their ears. Their hair color was rust-brown, gold, silver-gray, and mixed. Also, their bodies were streamlined like seals' bodies, as these aliens were originally amphibian. (See chapter 2, "Aboard the Alien Spacecraft," in *UFO . . . Contact from Planet Iarga: A Report of the Investigation.* Paraphrased pp. 27–28)

Iargans could die if they fell just six feet; thus, they had thick skulls, heavy muscles, and long arms. (See chapter 2, "Aboard the Alien Spacecraft," in *UFO . . . Contact from Planet Iarga: A Report of the Investigation.* 35)

According to Stefan, "they lacked the sex signals of humans, such as full lips, earlobes, pointed nose, protruding female breast, and external male organs." (See chapter 2, "Aboard the Alien Spacecraft," in *UFO . . . Contact from Planet Iarga: A Report of the Investigation.* 30) According to Stefan, they took less pleasure from sex than humans do, and their reproductive drive came from love, not lust. (See chapter 2, "Aboard the Alien Spacecraft," in *UFO . . . Contact from Planet Iarga: A Report of the Investigation.* 30)

Culture

Nonmaterial Components of Culture

Values

Earthlings define culture as a society's game plan for living. It can also be considered as all of the things that are material (e.g., computers) and nonmaterial (e.g., beliefs) that a group of people create in order to help them to survive. Iargans define culture as "the measure through which a society caters to the least fortunate man. [It is] the measure in which the sick, invalid, old, or poor people are taken care of. In short, [it is] the measure of collective unselfishness." (See chapter 2, "Aboard the Alien Spacecraft," in *UFO . . . Contact from Planet Iarga: A Report of the Investigation.* 51)

It was unselfishness that made a race immortal. (See chapter 2, "Aboard the Alien Spacecraft," in *UFO . . . Contact from Planet Iarga: A Report of the Investigation.* 51) Love and friendship influenced their social structure, and, thus, they lived for the group and not for individuality. They did nearly everything in groups. They thought collectively. (See chapter 2, "Aboard the Alien Spacecraft," in *UFO . . . Contact from Planet Iarga: A Report of the Investigation.* 30)

Why was the focus on the group and not the individual? Having a paucity of land and having many people living on it, they had to think collectively, and do their activities in groups, in order to survive. Out of all possible ways of behaving/acting, Iargans identified the preferable means as identified by the following predominant values:

Justice—a necessary condition for *efficiency*. Efficiency was necessary for survival. For instance, if their housing were different (i.e., some had better places to live than others), this would indicate a difference in social status; *justice* would fail, and *efficiency* would be denied.

Efficiency—the basis for everything they did. They evaluated everything in terms of it. For example, they estimated the amount of land needed for raising food for the number of individuals they had. In contrast, Americans evaluate the amount of land needed for making a profit for an owner.

Freedom (Justice)—Iargans treated one another as equals (not just legally but economically too). This formed the basis for using things *efficiently,* thus rendering a physical and social environment workable. Survival resulted from achieving stability in their social and physical environment. At this point in their social development, individuals could exercise their *freedom.*

Love—for Iargans, this was what humans call "Christian love"; they cited love as a condition for cosmic integration. Only unselfish behavior that restored the original efficiency of the natural order could give an intelligent race the certainty of survival until cosmic integration occurred. (See chapter 3, "Planet Iarga," in *UFO . . . Contact from Planet Iarga: A Report of the Investigation.* 83)

On Earth, advertising's purpose is to create a desire for new things, thus rendering old but usable things obsolete. *Materialism* and *conspicuous consumption* drive America's capitalistic system. They create social status and social inequalities. For instance, on Earth, if one's possessions are newer than another's, the first person is viewed in a better (i.e., higher) position than the second person. Consequently, people defer more to the first individual than to the second. People compete with one another as they strive to get more possessions. Iargans, in contrast, obtained goods because they were usable and needed. Efficiency, not status, drove economic and social relations on Iarga.

Beliefs

Unselfishness was good for a group's immortal survival. Iargans did not conceive of a "personal" survival as we on Earth. They did, however, recognize individuals. They were not a colony of ants marching together. They believed the purpose of existing included the following:

1. Developing an individual identity, mostly through birth, living, and working.
2. Achieving immortality by use of talents in creating works that lived beyond the individual.
3. Choosing daily between selfishness and unselfishness, as this choice formed a godly, or ungodly, consciousness.

Iargans recognized the presence of good and evil in individuals. Improvement of a group's mentality over generations enabled it to become unselfish, which in turn enhanced its survival ability. The sanction for choosing one's bad side was that *re*incarnation would not happen. Travel, mixing races, and obedience to godly laws yielded a uniform legal system, worldwide order, and the end of nationalism. The planet was socially and economically organized as one unit.

Sex Roles

Equality between the sexes existed on Iarga, but males and females did different things. For instance, females raised children and did social work. Females were dominant because they played the most significant role in the development of children's mentality.[11] Also, females were not sex objects, and physical sex did not draw Iargans together. Respect, love, and mutual interests brought them together.

Language

The creature told Stefan that Iargans "spoke the language of all living species in the universe. Even a plant or an animal will understand it. This language was spoken on Earth before the Babylonia confusions of tongues. You don't hear words, but sounds that are directly reflected by your emotional structure, the life-field. Therefore, don't try to understand words, but listen to the reflections of your soul." (See chapter 2, "Aboard the Alien Spacecraft," in *UFO . . . Contact from Planet Iarga: A Report of the Investigation.* 25)

Humanity's language is useful for describing a material world. Alien language is useful for communicating with anything alive anywhere in the universe. "One listens not to words, but, rather, hears the reflections in one's soul." (See chapter 2, "Aboard the Alien Spacecraft," in *UFO . . . Contact from Planet Iarga: A Report of the Investigation.* 25)

Norms

Although no norms were cited, one can infer them from Iargan values. For instance, since they valued justice, it is not unreasonable to believe they had rules for "properly" conducting one's behavior with others.

Material Components of Culture

Transportation

Craft

As described, the spacecraft Stefan encountered six miles out at sea was fifty feet in diameter, with a three-foot-wide opening. The next day, when he entered the craft, he observed several chambers with a variety of equipment. He saw a control panel filled with colored lights and darting lines. There were walkways separated by vertical metal grills that reached the roof.

Other spaceships were beautiful, polished, and silver. There were streamlined discs about ninety feet in diameter, with a domed glass panel above. There were slots around the outside lower rim. Stefan said an antigravity machine caused dust to rise from the ground when the craft took off.

Trains

Iargans had three types of rail systems: passenger, cargo, and recreational. Generally, their rail system had slim, shiny, torpedo-shaped compartments, and their trains traveled at a very high rate of speed. The only moving part on a train was its doors, which opened and closed.

The rail system traveled between housing blocks. The railroad had six lanes with eight tracks on them. They had two levels, one above the other. The rail system transported one million beings per hour. Iargan trains were luxurious, shock-free, and silent. They offered breathtaking views of the landscape. They had an automated rail system, run by robots, and schedule-free due to its reliability. (See chapter 2, "Aboard the Alien Spacecraft," in *UFO . . . Contact from Planet Iarga: A Report of the Investigation.* 40–43)

They also had a transoceanic rail system supported on magnetic shoes. Adjustable cables anchored towers into the sea. Cargo trains ran without any Iargans needing to be aboard to operate them. They used hotel trains for holiday travel. Groups of twenty-five passengers would go together. How much did it cost? Nothing, since Iargans had no money in their society!

Also, there was a three-level road-and-rail system on land. The top level was a six-track rail system that carried long torpedoes. The four inside tracks were for fast, long-distance traffic, while the two outer tracks were for local traffic. The other two levels were for cars; the outer tracks were for slow, local traffic, and the inner tracks were for higher, longer distances. The stations were huge, cross-shaped buildings through which the car-train tracks passed in tunnels.

Housing

Their houses were part of "house rings," glass tanks built in the form of a ring, with an enclosed central area for recreation. (See chapter 3, "Planet Iarga," in *UFO . . . Contact from Planet Iarga: A Report of the Investigation.* 66–67) These units, nine hundred feet in diameter by three hundred feet high, were immense. Ten thousand beings lived within each ring. The individual houses were in the form of rectangles. They each were sixty square kilometers, equaling six thousand individuals per square kilometer.[12] Each house looked the same on the outside but not inside. (See chapter 2, "Aboard the Alien Spacecraft," in *UFO . . . Contact from Planet Iarga: A Report of the Investigation.* 38)

They showed Stephan a housing unit. Each house had a large entrance hall that opened into a gallery. Everyone passed through this area. On one side of a glass wall, there were showers for washing before entering the building. No one seemed to care that they could be seen showering. Each shower was a tube with a three-foot diameter. White foam emanated from the tube, making the individual look like a large "soapsuds man." After foaming, they watered down and air-dried themselves. Males and females wore sarongs around the bottom half of their bodies but left the top half naked.

The living quarters were sixty feet by sixty feet, with a huge glass wall running the entire length of the room. There was built-in furniture, small, intimate bedrooms, and bright colors throughout.

One wall had a large screen, while another had a shower. The ceiling had diffused orange lighting, and strange objects decorated walls. There was a table eighteen feet long by five feet wide, and it sat twenty-five beings. The table rose up into a wall when it was not in use. Two sliding panels in the wall opened to reveal a cupboard with compartments holding unknown equipment. Each being took something like a tray, and they ate after a man said something. The creatures held a golden spoon-like implement in one hand, and placed the other on the knee of the person next to them. They ate in silence as they listened to a male and a female who were not eating. After the meal, they threw their arms around one another and stood together briefly. They then cleaned up, and the table retracted into the floor. There were no towels or dishcloths used in the cleanup process. Warm air dried everything.

The recreational area found in the center of the housing ring was about three hundred yards in diameter. It was a huge garden with tropical-looking plants and flowers. A rock garden and flowers surrounded a central pillar. Streams and waterfalls gave way to ponds and tanks with strange colored fish in them. Iargan children swam in these water places. (Stefan remembered the Iargan amphibian past.) Galleries ran on the inside of each floor.

A huge machine in the basement, where cars parked, drew heat out from the ground and distributed it throughout a building. Agricultural areas used garbage and sewage so there was none in the building. The next floors underground were offices, workshops, and production workplaces. To reduce the numbers of Iargans who traveled to work, they worked from home.

Technology

Iargan trains lasted a long time to conserve natural resources. They had no moving parts, as having them meant things wore out and had to be replaced. Once again, these beings valued efficiency: the transportation systems on Iarga were five times greater in speed than those on Earth. (See chapter 2, "Aboard the Alien Spacecraft," in *UFO . . . Contact from Planet Iarga: A Report of the Investigation.* 41)

Dress

Spacecraft crew members wore something resembling a uniform. It was dark blue in color. It had silky overalls with three-quarter-length sleeves and a deep V-neck. Part of the uniform was a white shirt with an old-fashioned high collar around the back of the neck. These uniforms had a broad, gold-colored belt around the waist. A symbol looking like an atom decorated the V-neck piece.

Average Iargans wore clothes, but it seemed to Stefan that they wore them more for decoration than anything else. A large cloth piece with a hole in its middle fell over their heads, fastened by a broad belt at the waist. They left their arms and the sides of their bodies uncovered. Their attire also included silky pants, tightened at the ankles and worn underneath the top cloth. Females wore this while on holiday.

Social Stratification

No social stratification existed on Iarga. They treated one another as equals.

Social Institutions

Schools and Hospitals

These institutions were on the top floor of housing units. Four screens in the middle of a classroom with four walls showed a day's lesson. Radiation transmitted the real information. A teacher sat behind the four screens, acting as an observer. Education continued until an Iargan was fifteen or sixteen years old, and then he or she moved on to advanced work.

There were two types of hospitals: one was at a house, and the other was a "real" hospital. Computers monitored patients and dealt with their maladies. The computer dealt with all the needs for each patient, such as administering medication, calling relatives, providing entertainment, and so on.

Farming

Stefan reported on the farming process. First, a machine using two U-shaped blades cut a strip of land into two layers. Second, a deadly ray sterilized the strip. Third, the strip received a spray with a muddy-looking fertilizer, which turned and returned to the furrow. Fourth, a row of fast-moving gooseneck-type pipes planted seeds for the next harvest. Finally, the machine rolled the surface flat and covered it with a transparent layer. Stefan said it looked like a dance floor when completed. It was an automated process.

Economy

The production of goods and services was in the hands of a very few huge companies called "trusts." Trusts had millions of employees working over the entire planet. There were two types of trusts: primary (distributed directly to consumers), and secondary (which supplied the primary ones).

Money did not exist, and nothing needed payment. Consumers registered what they used into a computer, and took only what was rightfully theirs. Expensive items, such as boats and cars, were "hired." They called this "the right of acquisition." They registered less-expensive items because of efficiency issues. Registration was for life, and so it was the closest thing to individual ownership that existed on the planet. Iargans registered the total value of an article for consumption and public service, and then the individual had a "right of use." There were no surpluses; individuals took only what they needed.

Iargans controlled expenditures, not income. Legally, all goods remained the property of the trusts that supplied them. They designed goods to last a very long time. (According to the book, insurance companies and repair shops did not do very well on Iarga.) Trusts worked on a cost-price basis. The cost of continuation replaced profit. Improved and expanded production was necessary. Automation directed production in factories, which were star-shaped. Railroad cars brought raw material to each star point.

They took Stefan to two automated factories. One produced cars, and the other made transoceanic rail bridges. There were two joined production lines in the middle of the factory. The factory only needed a few workers in the production process because of the automation. A machine a little over half a mile long, produced goods by means of its huge metal claw. This claw created cars from raw material, at the rate of one every twenty seconds! They said the factory produced 4,500 cars per day.[13]

Goods were meant to last for eternity! Iargans did this for efficiency; consequently, their orientation was for the future, and neither the past nor the present mattered, unlike the importance accorded to these on Earth. In an effort to accomplish efficiency, the Iargans placed a factory containing a monster-machine on-site.

Social Structure of Iargan Economic System

The Iargan economic system did not have private ownership of property, and, therefore, was not a capitalist system in this respect. There were divisions and branches to their organizational structure, and there were vast distances between them.

There was a head (i.e., president) for each of their trusts. This individual was a member of the production group of the world government. Trusts competed with one another, and the law of supply and demand determined prices. The "ura" was a standard work hour, and it was the basis for computing cost price. Availability of natural resources did not determine cost because these resources were free. For each article, price was equal to production time.

The efficiency of the working population was "welfare effiency [sic]." (See chapter 3, "Planet Iarga," in *UFO . . . Contact from Planet Iarga: A Report of the Investigation.* 65) When this figure was 100 percent, the total working population took part in the direct production process of goods and services, with the highest attainable level of automation, possible quality, and durability. (See chapter 3, "Planet Iarga," in *UFO . . . Contact from Planet Iarga: A Report of the Investigation.* 65) Three factors determined this figure:

1. The Occupation Factor—the percentage of the working population involved in the direct production of goods and services (advertising, accounting, etc., would not be in this category).
Iarga = 90 percent; Earth = 30–40 percent
2. The Production Effectivity [sp] Factor—expressed in terms of the relationship to the maximum possible at the moment. Everything that can be automated is classed as 100 percent. Earth = about 50 percent lower
3. The Quality Factor—determined the effect of particular goods or investments on prosperity. A product lasting twice as long as another had twice the effect on prosperity. Repair time diminished the effect.

(See chapter 3, "Planet Iarga," in *UFO … Contact from Planet Iarga: A Report of the Investigation.* 65–69)

Welfare Effiency [sic] was equal to (1) x (2) x (3) (above).

Intelligent races = 70 percent (The Universal Economic System)
Average Industrialized Countries = 7 or 9 percent
(Earth had many professions that consumed prosperity instead of creating it; for instance, advertising.) (See chapter 3, "Planet Iarga," in *UFO . . . Contact from Planet Iarga: A Report of the Investigation.* 68–70)

Although competition existed on Iarga, it did not create inequality. Materialism and conspicuous consumption were unheard of on this planet. Iargans made things to last an eternity, and they used these items because they were necessary. There were two worldwide consumer organizations responsible for market research. Goods and services were not for status-making. They served a more practical reason: Efficiency. Factories produced goods efficiently in order to avoid misusing natural resources, and there was no advertising. They educated their populace to buy things based on need. The Iargan creature told Stefan that higher-intelligence planets did not concern themselves with money, possession, or payment. Their aim was to free individuals from material influence and motivation.

Religion

There was nothing about religion mentioned in the Iargan book. Their entire social existence seemed to be religious. They noted only one goal for their society. It was perfection.

Iargans claimed "by mutual love so that the whole race, including the slower ones, were capable of taking part in the 'Omni-creative integration process.' This longing for absolute values creates a mutual bond, so dominant, that a situation of collective consciousness replaces the individual." (See chapter 4, "Iargan Society," in *UFO . . . Contact from Planet Iarga: A Report of the Investigation.* 96)

The Christian (Protestant and Roman Catholic) faith professes in their Nicene Creed[14] that the church (i.e., its people) is the body of Christ. On Iarga, its inhabitants (i.e., its "people") were Iarga. Could a latent function of this book on Iarga be that it reflected the secularization of the European Christian Church in the Netherlands?

Social Problems

Overpopulation

As previously mentioned, the Iargans organized their houses into a rectangular configuration. Each rectangle was ten kilometers long and contained thirty-six rings. (See chapter 2, "Aboard the Alien Spacecraft," in *UFO . . . Contact from Planet Iarga: A Report of the Investigation.* 39) Thus, 360,000 beings live in a rectangle. (This is equivalent to the population of Wichita, Kansas!) Approximately six thousand individuals lived within an area of roughly half a square mile. That is dense, but it is *not* unheard of on Earth. Perhaps the Iargan principle of efficiency may be a lesson for urban planners on Earth!

Social Change

There was no mention of social change on Iarga. However, the Iargan creature did refer to this concept as it applied to Earth. He mentioned how Earth's social development lagged behind its technological progress. (See conclusion that follows for elaboration.)

Conclusion

Luckily for us, Stefan chose to learn about Iargan society, rather than having these beings' technology described to him. He chose to be a *social* scientist instead of a *physical* scientist. Having made this decision, he brought us data from which we constructed an understanding of what a society on another planet looked like.

Stefan's contact with Iargans happened six miles out to sea. He jumped from his yacht to save what he thought was a person, and landed in three feet of water! He had landed on an alien spacecraft. Talk about culture shock! Unless it was a submerged submarine (he did not think it was), what could it be?

Stefan's first contact with alien beings off the coast of the Netherlands showed us immediately that these creatures had advanced technology. The alien claimed his origin was another solar system. For a craft to fly from one solar system to another not only exceeded the limits of human technology, it also superseded people's wildest imaginings.

Neither race was value neutral in their estimation of the other. Aliens and humans judged one another. Consequently, they acted as cultural absolutists. Aliens judged humans to be inferior, and humans deemed aliens to be technologically superior. Therefore, humans and aliens expressed ethnocentric views. Apparently, when beings from across the cosmos met each other, one of their first acts was to judge one another.[15]

The creature claimed humans were *not* intellectually inferior to Iargans. Rather, Iargans claimed that humans were less technologically developed. If both were intellectual equals, why was Iargan technology so much more advanced than humans? There are two possible reasons for this: (1) their species were harder workers than humans, so they moved further along in development than earthlings did; and/or (2) their civilization was older than Earth's, and, consequently, they had more time to develop their technology than humans had.

The creature seemed to be very concerned about consequences accrued from the gap between human technological and social development. He noted that human technological progress exceeded humanity's social advancement. In other words, he noted the effects of culture lag on social progress. Simply stated, culture lag impeded social progress on Earth.

The example the alien gave was the money humans spent on Mars probes versus the attention humanity paid to discrimination among fellow humans, such as blacks, Asians, and Native Americans. As this cultural lag continued, social power would be unequally distributed, and the gap between the haves and the have-nots would widen. Such discrimination, according to the alien, weakened a society's/planet's social evolution toward *social stability* and, therefore, toward *cosmic integration.*

As Stefan examined the material components of an alien culture further, he was baffled. For such a technologically advanced spacecraft, material articles found on it seemed primitive. For instance, Stefan found a "normal-looking chair with metal frame and leather upholstery," as well as, "reels, drums, cables, and metal doors." (See chapter 2, "Aboard the Alien Spacecraft," in *UFO . . . Contact from Planet Iarga: A Report of the Investigation.* 25) Were there primitive articles (by humanity's standards) on this advanced spacecraft, or was Stefan's language inadequate for describing such foreign-looking objects? Was what he saw so different that his words failed him? Was this an example of a problem of ineffability (i.e., inability to describe in words what one sees)?

The problem of ineffability rose again when considering how creatures from different solar systems communicated. Human contact with an alien creature raised three issues: First, if the alien world was vastly different from Earth, how could human words describe this other world? Second, human words have changed over time. Once, people used words from magic, folklore, and religion to describe the nature of things; now, people are more apt to apply words from science. Third, scientific words effectively described a material world but not a nonmaterial one.

First, the Iargan creature said communication among living things throughout the cosmos (i.e., humanoids, animals, plants) and "humans before the Babylonia confusion of tongues" took place via a universal language. (See chapter 2, "Aboard the Alien Spacecraft," in *UFO . . . Contact from Planet Iarga: A Report of the Investigation.* 25) It was a language of emotions, not words. One did not listen to words, but, rather, heard the reflection in one's soul. (See chapter 2, "Aboard the Alien Spacecraft," in *UFO . . . Contact from Planet Iarga: A Report of the Investigation.* 25) The alien said it was similar to, but not the same as, thought transference. What was he talking about?

What the alien said was so far outside people's normative frame of understanding that his words were incomprehensible. His statement causes one to consider the fundamentals of communication and understanding. How could people comprehend the alien's reality with human words? People may not understand because human language describes the human world. If the alien's world was so vastly different from Earth's, how could human words describe it, and, consequently, how could earthlings understand it?[16]

Second, humanity's frames for understanding the nature of experience have changed from using magic, folklore, and religion to employing science. Originally, societies consisted of hunters and gatherers; later, they were made up of farmers (i.e., agricultural societies). In the past, things seen at night were imps, goblins, and demons, because the language of those days referred to magic, folklore, and religion. When society became industrial (and, later, computer-informational), science (and technology) became the dominant form for explaining the nature of experience. Now these night-sky entities are aliens who arrived in technologically advanced spacecraft.

Third, after changing to the scientific method, people came to see this approach was good for understanding the material world, but not the nonmaterial one. This method collected and analyzed data, but how could it examine the reflection in one's soul? (See chapter 2, "Aboard the Alien Spacecraft," in *UFO . . . Contact from Planet Iarga:*

A Report of the Investigation. 25) In fact, scientists argued nonmaterial elements were not valid items to be studied within the scientific method.

The point is, as societies changed the words they used for describing things, their world changed too. When humans were in small groups and clans, people knew one another in personal ways (Gemeinschaft organization). Today, people act impersonally with one another (Gesellschaft organization). The frame of human stories changed in regard to the things people see in the sky. Once those entities were gods, angels, and creatures riding on carpets, but now they are intelligent beings from other worlds. They arrive on Earth in technologically advanced supertransports; that is, in craft commensurate with the temper of the times.

Given this perspective, perhaps those prominent in the UFO community constitute a social movement, the latent function of which is to extend the ancient frames of reference that magic, folklore, and religion put forth in the past and blend them with the scientific advancements of today. The UFO phenomenon (with the NDE)[17] may be viewed as a cauldron. Ancient frames of understanding the nature of things blend with the contemporary frames in this mix. Finally, the mystical joins with the scientific as humans peer out into the vast unknown above their heads and seek an understanding of it all.

Book #4
UFO Contact from Planet Ummo:
The Incredible Truth (volume 2)

[AUTHOR'S NOTE: The numbers in parentheses found below refer to pages in *UFO Contact from Planet Ummo*.]

Incident Described

Between February 5 and 7, 1934, a Norwegian ship off the coast of Newfoundland conducted experiments in communication over long distances. Their radio waves escaped into the ionosphere.

Fourteen years later (1948), these waves found their way to Ummo. The broadcast was long enough for the Ummites to obtain Earth's coordinates. According to the author of *UFO from Planet Ummo: The Incredible Truth* (volume 2), the Ummites recorded this date as their first contact from earthlings.

Ummites landed on Earth for the first time on March 28, 1950. It happened thirteen kilometers (just over eight miles) from Digne, France. Other earthly arrivals occurred on February 6, 1966: (1) two "brothers" near Erivan, Soviet Union; (2) two "brothers" near Madrid, Spain; and (3) three "brothers" near Townsville, Queensland Territory, Australia. (29)

Although the events of this alien contact happened in France, a Spaniard, Antonia Ribera, wrote the account. He began studying contacts from Ummo, and when "they" found out, the Ummites contacted him. According to Ribera, they had been coming to Earth in spacecraft that were forty feet in diameter, and they were *not* the only ETs visiting us. Ummite exploration of Earth began in Spain in the mid-1960s, and communication with them had gone on until about 1984. They came in teams of sixty to eighty members. In 1967, and again in 1973, they left Earth because they feared that humans would "blow ourselves up" in a nuclear war. In 1967, the Ummites[18] sent a description of their culture to one of their contacts in Madrid, Don Manuel Campo; this was for the purpose of gaining knowledge of Earth, but *not* to convert earthlings to the Ummite way of life.

Planet's Environment

According to the Ummites, their planet is slightly over fourteen light-years (864.6 trillion miles) away from Earth. (25) Ummo had an elliptical orbit around its star, Iumma. (233–234) An Ummo day is just over thirty hours long. (26) Their sun was a dwarf star, meaning it had average or low luminosity, mass, and size.[19] According to Antonio, it might be a Wolf 424 star.[20] The planet was nearly 62 percent water and had one continent (233) with many great lakes. (26) They called their largest lake "Little Sea of God." (26) Ummo had small mountains.

A few of them had volcanoes that emitted brilliant columns of incandescent combinations of methane, pentane, and oxygen. (26–27)

Demography: Aliens' Characteristics

Ummites described themselves as an "old people" (208) dispersed into many social groups throughout their planet before they unified under a monocratic government. (208) There was one race on Ummo. Ummites had ten fingers (like humans). Their morphology was similar to that of earthlings, but with slight differences. For instance, their phonetic organ atrophied during adolescence, which deprived them of the ability to speak. (28) However, they used an artificial device that helped them articulate. Apparently, Ummites had stages of life similar to those of humans, insofar as they acknowledged an adolescent period. There were no racial differences among Ummites because there was less variation of their chromosomes; this was the result of Ummo having an atmosphere that was more protected than Earth's. (29) Ummite sexual morphology and endocrine mechanisms were similar to humans. (184) Also, there was a narrower variation among animals on Ummo as compared to animals on Earth. (234)

Reason Aliens Made Contact with Humans

The aliens' purpose in contacting humans was to learn Earth's languages and observe earthlings' ways of life. In 1966, Ummites came to Earth to study and analyze Earth's culture. (30) They would not interfere with Earth's progress because of two norms: (1) "a cosmic moral prohibits a paternalistic attitude toward planetary social systems, which must grow gradually on their own." (234–235) Furthermore, (2) their intervention into humanity's world would cause incalculable interruptions to earthlings, and would contaminate the scientific study of humans by Ummites. (235)

Culture

Ummites said their level of science and technological development was much more advanced than Earth's, but humanity's art (painting, sculpture, and especially music) was superior to theirs. They claimed that Ummo was older than Earth, and that Ummites had reached an "elevated level" of civilization.

Nonmaterial Components of Culture

Beliefs

Ummites did not fear offering their perspective on earthly practices. Here again, an alien species, acting as cultural absolutists, found it comfortable passing judgment on earthly actions. In this instance, the aliens (Ummites) warned about the threat of nuclear war. (35) However, they saw hope in what they called "the three currents of Earth philosophy [that were] most important. These were Christianity, Marxism, and Existentialism." (36) They recognized that the goal for Earth, as well as all higher civilizations, was *integration*. They called it "UNITARY Nucleization [sic]." (36) They predicted the integration of economics, politics, religion, and philosophy on Earth sometime in its future. (36)

Ummite beliefs included the following:

> *The Nature of the Cosmos*—Ummites know (not believe) that there are multiple universes, not just one. In fact, they hold that there are an infinite number of pairs of universes. (198) Twin worlds cannot come into contact with each other because of differences in time and space between them. However, they do influence one another. (199) The Ummite universe and its twin operate by basic biogenetic laws. These laws regulate the structure and evolution of all flora and fauna. (203)

WOA (God)—Ummites affirm the God exists. They call God "the Generator" (WOA). (200) WOA created/generated their universe. The number of realities that exist is equal to the number of non-incompatible ideas in the mind of God. (200)

Origin of Humans—"humans were formed by four integrated factors whose association is necessary for humans to live." (203) They were: (1) a collective soul; (2) a soul (the Ummite book's claim is similar to the Roman Catholic religion's view); (3) a connection between the soul and human body (the soul is located in the human encephalic mass); (4) the human body has ten dimensions (three of them define volume, six express mass, and one represents time). (204)

Values

Ummite values included the following:

Modesty—Ummites undressed in the dark, and they showed their naked bodies only to their spouses. Single females were permitted to flirt.

Respect and *Love*—this referred to all Ummites. Those who did not show respect and love were viewed as "failures" by other Ummites. (214)

Abstract and *Rational Thinking*—those displaying a high degree of these traits attended a university.

Norms

Because Ummites value modesty, a doctor, upon seeing a female patient, injected a chemical that covers her skin. Not following this norm yielded humiliation for females. (185)

Also, Ummites expected individuals to live at their respective levels of aptitude. If they did, they received an appropriate reward. (This payment was not in money because money did not exist on Ummo.) (197)

Psychobiological laws matched males and females for copulation. (215) If they did not follow this law, the sanction was that their practice would create a "disturbance in the harmony of one's community of which they would be held responsible." (215)

Status

Psychosomatic aptitude determined position in society. (196) If individuals demonstrated superiority in the cerebral cortex, they went to university.

Rituals

On May 29, 1950, six members of the expeditionary crew left Earth, joining twenty-four other Ummites who boarded three craft to leave. (67–68) They bid farewell to their compatriots by placing a hand on the chest of another. Although they said nothing, their eyes conveyed their feelings to one another. (68)

Courting

When Ummite males reached the age of fifteen and a half years, they selected their partners. They then submitted their selection to educational authorities who used a computer to examine the candidates. (185) The device measured each couple's physiological and mental compatibility. If the result was positive, the male made his proposal. The female was usually younger, and not had her first menstruation. If she accepted his proposal, the couple waited until she was biologically ready for parenthood. They could not communicate with each other, and if they did, the engagement would be broken.

When the female reached puberty, she celebrated at a party with fellow female classmates and friends. After she announced her intentions to her friends, she notified her "boyfriend." If she agreed to be married, the couple engaged in an educational process to prepare them for marriage. They learned sexual, religious, and social planning for their marital union. They each received an intimate biography of their partner, as well as their psychophysiological characteristics. After this, they could touch one another, but not on their erogenous zones. The purpose of this was to strengthen a spiritual bond that would prepare them for a religious/legal bond. (186)

Gender Roles

Wives could express their opinions, even though they submitted to their husbands. Males and females were treated equally in the workplace. At work, females achieved supervisory positions, but males had difficulty accepting them in these roles. Eventually, the males accepted the females with integrity and discipline. Females showed their bodies only to their husbands, but a female could "capture the attention of a single male before her engagement." (184)

Age Roles

Age began at the time of conception (not birth).

Language

They had a double language (by means of sequential repetition of various vocables [sp]), wherein they expressed two ideas simultaneously. (27)

Time was the period that transpired for the mass of an isotope of TORIO WAEELEWIWWOATR to be reduced by 50 percent. (27)

Mathematics had a system of twelve (not ten).

Material Components of Culture

Spacecraft

Ummite spacecraft was a little over thirteen meters (43.2 feet) in diameter. (29) Three legs extended from the spacecraft upon landing. (29) Magnetism propelled the craft, which appeared and disappeared in an instant. (30) The spacecraft still existed, but when it disappeared, it went into another system of dimensions. (61, 63) Spacecraft emitted an orange luminosity upon taking off and landing. This luminosity decontaminated germs that may have attached to their craft.

Technology

Ummite communication systems were quite advanced. They were able to make contact with intelligent species in other galaxies, such as Andromeda. (45) However, these technologies had limitations. For example, telepathic communication with humans failed over vast distances.[21] Ummites received a message from a planet six thousand years after it destroyed itself with plasma weapons. (45–46)

Ummites acknowledged their inferiority in photographic techniques (as compared to humans), explaining that this was because they (Ummites) had difficulty understanding how to control light for the reproduction of an image. (191)

Housing

Ummite houses were tubular structures that extended above and below ground. Each structure was the same. The principles of conservation and distribution of consumable products informed their construction. (50) Ummites manufactured and/or prepared food in industrial plants. Neutrons purified their food. Families received their food via home delivery from the industrial food factories.

Dress

Ummites wore skintight brown clothing while on expeditions to other planets. The clothing was brown for camouflage purposes. When Pierre, a human boy, first saw these beings in his father's cow field, he merely thought they were foreigners because of their strange dress. However, the Ummite "brothers" thought the boy knew that they were aliens. Later, these same Ummites wore human clothing in order to blend into human society.

Social Stratification

Ummites had a stratified society, as Antonio made references throughout the book about individuals in unequal positions. For example, while discussing the role of females in earlier days, Ummites said that a female could get into a "hierarchical position" (189); later, they explained that they were able "to neutralize the privileges of class." (197) Also, some Ummites held official (upper-class) positions, while others were "slave laborers." (208) Finally, the Ummites stated, "If in the social scale . . . you are superior to your brother, and he must submit to you, do not humiliate him. ..." (214) Assignment to a position did not depend "on property ownership, genetic inheritance, or muscular strength but rather aptitude of mind and in spiritual equilibrium of the individuals." (217)

Social Institutions

Marriage

Children notified their parents of their marriage intentions. Parents could not interfere with a couple's decision, unless the children were younger than approximately fifteen and a half years old. Religious ministers oversaw a simple religious/legal ceremony. A minister, educational authorities involved with the couple, parents, and the couple's siblings attended the ceremony. Rules permitted only twelve individuals to attend. After the ceremony, the couple went to an adjacent bedroom while the others at the ceremony went to a nearby room to wait. The husband emerged, while relatives respectfully greeted him. The wife remained in bed for four thousand UIW (one UIW equaled a little over three Earth minutes; thus, approximately eight and a half days). (187)

The married couple selected their home and a transportation vehicle. They received a "salary." (As stated previously, no money existed on Ummo. Essentially, Ummites got credit based on their intellectual capacity, and their contribution to labor since their educational days.) They worked for the state.

The purposes of marriage were conjugal love and bearing children. Wives submitted to their husbands, and married life hummed along. They did not have children for egotistical reasons, and, if they did, the government would confiscate the children, and the couple would be shunned by relatives and friends. Because society matched couples for mental, intellectual, and spiritual complementarities, divorce was rare.

Government

Initially, Ummo had a monocratic government elected by a proclamation of chiefs of population. (192) Although they developed slowly, the seeds of tyranny evolved as well. The daughter of an official (NA-312) proclaimed herself "absolute chief of Ummo" at the age of thirteen years old. (192) She did have great intellectual ability. When she was just a little past fifteen years old, she promulgated twelve laws (or decrees) that declared her "proprietor of all beings on Ummo." She then went on to initiate cult rituals, and also to establish scientific investigations as Ummo's supreme goal. (194) Furthermore, she sacrificed males on the altar of science, torturing scientists who did not make contributions to their profession. Male and female Ummites of all ages, even children, who did not display a level of intelligence, became guinea pigs for experimentation. (194) When this self-appointed female ruler died, the population rose up in opposition to science. They burned labs, and Ummo evolved from an autocracy to polycracy.

Ummites selected a ruling group comprised of four members chosen by psychophysiological examinations. (28, 234) This group was called the "Counsel General of Ummo." Sociometric principles promulgated laws that regulated the Ummites. (28) Neither age nor race discrimination existed. The four council members were selected from among 120 young Ummites who were at least thirteen and a half years old and intellectually brilliant. These four governed and made rules that lasted sixty-four years. (196)

Economics

In their "old days," millions of male and female Ummites became exiles. They worked as slave laborers or were used in biological experiments.[22] Labor was coordinated by efficient group discipline, and there was no money on Ummo (as previously stated). A computer (or, "electronic brains") processed transactions. (28, 234) Ummites did not value things (e.g., food and transportation), because supply exceeded demand. (234) The ground and space were public places.

Religion

As stated, Ummites believed in God (WOA), and they considered themselves a very religious society. (28) They asserted that they had *scientific proof* for the existence of the soul (BUAWAA). (28) (234) They claimed knowledge of a factor (constituted of atoms of krypton located in the encephalic mass [234]) that connected humans to the "Adimensional Soul." (28–29) They maintained that their religion was much like human Christianity. (29)

Rigorous scientific arguments supported concepts about the beginning of the cosmos; such arguments did not include the philosophical speculation that existed in similar earthly concepts. Again, Ummites *knew* that there were multiple pairs of universes, not just one universe (as we believe on Earth). Ummites heard from another planet, Koldas, that it was the parallel planet to Ummo in a different universe. (That meant Earth also had a "twin" in another universe.) Ummites further held God (WOA) generated the universe.

Ummites claimed that there was a redeemer (UMMOWOA) whose characteristics were remarkably similar to those of Jesus. However, whereas Christ died on a cross, UMMOWOA died on an "operating" table (created for purposes of torture). Regardless, both were martyred public figures. (206) UMMOWOA gave charismatic speeches to the "humble uncultured classes" (210) during the reign of terror (the self-proclaimed rule of the official's daughter). UMMOWOA sought to unify the population to throw off the tyranny that enslaved them. After several efforts, he surrendered himself to the police. They turned him over to the officials, who satisfied their sadistic tendencies by torturing him. (211) His body vanished on the torture (i.e., "operating") table. (211) When Ummites realized the parallels between UMMOWOA and Christ, they were amazed. (212) Over time, the Ummites mastered a synthesis among science, technology, and spirituality.

Military

A military existed on Ummo, at least during the reign of the official's daughter, but there were no details given about this.

Social Problems

Sexual Practices (Masturbation, Prostitution, Contraception, and Homosexuality)

Specialists repressed the masturbatory practices of children, using an electrostatic device on the children's genitals in order to curtail this "vice." These specialists claimed that such "treatment" did not adversely affect sexuality later in life. Although 82.5 percent of children stopped using this practice (177), a number of them became impotent in later life because of the use of this device during childhood.

Ummites claimed that if individuals reached their reproductive years but remained celibate, they *violated* divine laws. (178) They had severe psychosocial controls to dissuade morbid eroticism.

They permitted prostitution in one's earlier years, and their chiefs/governors regulated the trafficking of females. During the rule of the official's daughter, young female Ummites who reached puberty were ordered to become pregnant. Only wives and daughters of high functionaries were exempt. Officials examined young females to see if they complied with the practice. If they didn't, they received a death sentence. Many committed suicide. Hypersexed females continued in prostitution, but, after many years, this syndrome began to diminish, aided by religious practices. (179–80)

Rational thinking, the use of the scientific method, and the technology generated by it yielded family-planning practices on Ummo. There were consultations with the religious ministry, as well as their computer network. Together, these estimated the pros and cons of genetic factors, professional situation, parental intelligence, and emotional state prior to Ummites engaging in procreation.

No birth control devices were necessary because Ummites had control over their reproductive cycles. They knew the exact moment a female could conceive (see detailed explanation below). A couple would communicate their decision to mate to those living with them, including their children. When that time arrived, a couple performed a ceremony, which included a celebration of the "new being that would be born." (181) While engaged in the sex act, if a couple generated sounds, they would be of affection more than physical pleasure. Only genitals, breasts, bellies, and buttocks were erogenous. Human erogenous areas, such as muscles, feet, and face, were not erogenous. Kissing did nothing for Ummites. Nudity was shocking to them, so they undressed in the dark.

There was a sanction against artificial contraception on Ummo, because such measures were not necessary. (181) Every Ummite household had a machine called IWOUAXOO, which detected the exact moment a female conceived. (181)

Ummites considered homosexuality an "abnormality," and they treated it in adolescence during coeducational sessions. (185)

Torture

Torture took place during the time of the official's daughter's reign. Examples included cutting off her servant's ear, as well as slashing off the breast of her mathematics teacher. Also, she castrated one of her mother's favorite military chiefs. (209)

Social Change

As in any society with a long history, social change was virtually inevitable. Ummites acknowledged, for instance, that the role of females was changing, but they did not go into detail on this point. (184) Also, they described how their beliefs had evolved from a monocratic government to a tyranny, and, finally to the use of scientific principles for the purpose of taking action. (192)

Conclusion

The book on Ummo was unusual in that it *reversed the tables* of analysis from earthlings studying aliens to aliens studying earthlings. People's study of "other worlds" included such places as Acart and Iarga, but in the case of Antonio's report, aliens came to Earth to study humans. Essentially, humans were the "other world"! Individuals saw an alien's bird's-eye view of earthlings. Humans saw how aliens understood people. It was like hearing a pride of lions that tagged humans for study describe their observations of how people lived.

For instance, Ummites first thought that earthlings made smoke from tubes that they held between their lips (i.e., the practice of smoking). (44) Also, their first examination of the Earth's crust revealed "tubular conduits," which later they discovered were roads and railroads. Their first detection of aircraft happened near the Bahamas Islands, and from this observation they determined human's (low) level of technology. (47) Their first observation of urban centers and industries happened as they saw the Republic of Helvetica in Switzerland. (47) Finally, from the sky, they saw concentrations of flora (forests and plantations) and floating structures (ships in the Atlantic Ocean). (47)

What if the Ummites used our diagram-for-social-living as a framework for understanding human culture? What would their analysis look like? The following section provides an answer to these questions.

Earth (as Viewed by Ummites)

Incident Described

The first problem Ummites had was where to land on Earth. They did not want to draw attention to themselves, and they needed time to adjust. They thought landing in a remote area was their best choice, but they feared humans might live in subterranean areas. As it turned out, no one detected the Ummites, and after awhile, they developed a subterranean observatory. (60)

Their first view of a human was on the streets of Monteux, a village in Switzerland. (47) They were encouraged to discover that humans had a civilization. (Apparently, culture shock is *not* exclusively a human occurrence!) Ummites hypothesized the extent of human development, and they were eager to study earthlings in order to test out their hypotheses. (As you read this, consider how it might feel to be such a "guinea pig"!)

Ummites began their study of human beings by examining pictures of them. The first picture had "individuals of different sex [sic] and age [sic] walking among buildings." (48) The Ummites conducting this study claimed that the faces and body features made it possible for them to identify some humans as females. Ummites later described an "abundance of cranial hair" on the heads of human women, but they originally thought this might be "some fibrous material over the head." (48) They also noted the differences in busts of human males and females, but this confused the Ummites because men and women on Earth seemed to wear similar dress on their legs. (48–49) (Understanding earthlings' mode of dress was valuable to

Ummites. They wished to blend in, so they had to figure out the proper (i.e., normative) mode of dress for each sex.)

Ummites' first observations of Earth and its artifacts were sometimes incorrect. For instance, they thought homes were factories. They mistakenly interpreted the large vertical tubes located near or on top of these buildings (chimneys), as well as those attached to vehicles (exhaust pipes), as constructions that expelled factory gases. Moreover, they thought humans could *not* live with oxygen and nitrogen because of the pervasive presence of these two gases.

When the "brothers" entered a human dwelling for the first time, they took numerous objects, such as money, clothing, a calendar, and lightbulbs. Their intrusion was actually far more extensive than this. They conducted physical exams on the married couple who lay sleeping in their bed throughout the Ummites visit. They took samples of perspiration from their armpits and lower abdomens of the man and woman; hair from their heads, arms, pubic regions, and legs; pieces of their eyelashes; and samples of nasal and vulvar secretions.

Ummites stayed on Earth from 1950 to 1984 (at least). During that time, they collected human artifacts in an effort to understand how earthlings lived. They contacted some high- and low-ranking officials of major countries on Earth.

Planet's Environment

Adaptation

Ummites had to ascertain an understanding of Earth's atmosphere and food in order to survive. First, they analyzed components of the atmosphere to detect its ingredients, finding them compatible with the Ummite atmosphere. Likewise, they found that the composition of Earth and its animal life agreed with their digestive system. Thus, the Ummites concluded that they could survive on Earth.

Animals

On the second day of exploration (March 30, 1967), Ummites came upon eight "vertibrate [sic] animals with sharply pointed protruberances [sic] coming out of the top of the cranium." (72) The Ummites were about 1,100 feet away from the animals. Ummo had no such creatures. It turned out they were cows with halters on them.

Demography: Aliens' Characteristics

Although the Ummite expeditionary team prepared for landing on Earth, much of what they saw was foreign to them. They previewed pictures of humans, animals, and the like, but when they came in contact with animate (e.g., cows) and inanimate (e.g., houses) objects for the first time, the experience disoriented them. (Apparently, culture shock happens to aliens too!)

The team came upon what they thought was an adolescent boy in a field. He was attending to creatures with protrusions on top of their heads. The beings could not determine the boy's sex because his clothes covered him. The boy carried a yellow substance in his hand that had a dark product impregnated into it. (73) He ate both products while peering at the three "brothers." He spoke to the brothers, but getting no response from them, he moved closer and gestured to them by placing his hand on its side just above his eyebrow, after which he looked more attentive. (73) When the brothers did not respond, the boy left.

As mentioned previously, the boy's name was Pierre. (73) The yellow substance the boy held in his hand was bread, and the dark product was a sausage. Although the brothers thought Pierre was saluting them, he was merely shading his eyes from the sun.

Reason Aliens Made Contact with Humans

Again, Ummites came to Earth to study humans. They sought an understanding of humanity's culture. They accomplished gaining this understanding by hiding their presence from earthlings. When

Ummites shared their knowledge with humans, they did it to increase people's understanding of the universe, not to change humanity. Ummites were true social scientists. They sought *value neutrality* and *verstehen*. They did not want to influence how humans lived, nor did they want to understand people from their viewpoint. Truly, they were cultural anthropologists!

Cultural anthropologists attest that, though value neutrality and verstehen are notable goals, they are difficult to attain. If Ummites gave humans the cure to cancer, would humans not immediately implement it? It was worthwhile to seek an understanding of another culture from the point of view of that "other"; however, doing so was challenging. For instance, interpreting the meaning embedded in Marcel Duchamp's painting *Nude Descending a Staircase*[23] is difficult for the average human, let alone a being from another galaxy!

Culture

Nonmaterial Components of Culture

Socialization

Learning how a planet's intelligent beings live is a daunting task. Having an "insider" to aid in the process can be extremely helpful. Pierre, the son of the farmer who owned the cows, acted as the brothers' socializing agent. He provided the Ummite brothers (socializees) with basic knowledge for understanding humans, such as language syntax, dress patterns, and the fundamentals of daily living.

Language

Initially, from outer space, Ummites received short and long waves (Morse code) based on a binary system. When they arrived on Earth, they tried to communicate in this fashion, but the heterogeneous nature of humanity confused them at first. They detected visual images (TV) and thought this was another language. They found all of these communications puzzling, and they did not understand any of them. In the absence of understanding language, they could not comprehend anything about human culture.

Norms

The Ummite expedition to Earth enacted these norms:

> *Follow Orders*—Ummite males, however, had difficulty following orders from females, and those males younger than they.

> *Rigorous Discipline*—guided crew members on long intergalactic voyages; members of the expeditionary crew were volunteers.

Sanctions

Crew members who broke rules were stripped naked in front of their superiors. Humiliation stopped future infractions. More stringent sanctions included physical punishment and even death. (61)

Material Components of Culture

Housing

Ummites observed artificial structures (human homes), and realized they were the sources of the lights they saw from the sky at night. Also, a dominant, strange tower that they saw in Digne, France, turned out to be a Romanesque-style Catholic cathedral. They took samples from the cathedral's columns.

On April 24, 1950, Ummites entered a human's home for the first time (as described previously). (80) It was three o'clock in the morning. (81) Before entering, Ummite brothers scanned the building to detect the presence of humans. It was a dormitory occupied by workers and a married couple with three children. The Ummites anesthetized the people in their sleep. (81) The brothers took items for examination such as money, clothing, a calendar, and lightbulbs. They took these objects to their underground lab for analyses.

Document

The expedition brothers came across "fragments of yellowish-white sheets, flexible and crushed into wrinkles, and full of characters or symbols written by human beings. Three of them appeared soiled by fecal traces. A multitude of unknown flying animals were taking flight." (69) The sheets were in a field. The Ummites saw strange characters, sketches, and photographs on the pages. Additionally, they observed a human adult with two children in a picture on the paper. Another page had a picture of a human dressed in the classic style. They were extremely excited with this find, and began to hypothesize what it was.

One hypothesis they considered was that a human reader of the document may have gotten angry at what he read, and defecated onto it in protest. (69) What they actually saw was a newspaper soiled by dog feces and urine (i.e., yellow sheet), with flies (i.e., flying animals) stirring from the paper when the Ummites picked it up. This finding and their interpretation of its meaning demonstrated the difficulty of studying alien cultures. These aliens found such a common item as a newspaper mystifying, and discovered that deciphering its meaning was even more difficult.[24]

Social Institutions

Politics

The politics of intergalactic contact needed to be understood and implemented when Ummites landed on Earth. They originally thought they had to "play it low"; that is, to stay out of sight so as not to be discovered. They learned, however, that they could blend into human society. Consequently, they implemented a process of immersion into the human world. First, they established a team of six who descended to Earth. (55) This team consisted of:

1. A thirty-one-year-old (by Earth standards) male biologist who was the director of the expedition.
2. An eighteen-year-old male, still living on Earth, who was an expert in human psychobiology.
3. An eighteen-year-old female who was an expert in physics.
4. A seventy-eight-year-old male communications expert.
5. A twenty-two-year-old male sociologist (who died in an accident in what was then Yugoslavia).
6. A thirty-two-year-old female who was an expert in digestion diseases.

Next, they composed a letter from the UMMO Council General to the Council of the Chief of Earth's inhabitants. (56) The Ummites impressed the letter "upon a lamination of iron, carbon, and vanadium alloy, and carried a series of ideographic images representing human acts and gestures, combinations of geometric figure forms, and ciphers expressed in (the) language of a Binary System." (56)

Anticipating that earthly viruses, germs, and the like would be different from theirs, the Ummites wore protective equipment that incorporated a new plastic epidermis allowing respiration while also filtering biochemical agents. (57) It was a protective skin. (58) They carried necessary equipment to purify water. They had equipment for every bodily orifice, such as for ears, eyes, mouth, and anus. (59)

Ummites did not describe the following pertaining to Earth: *social stratification, social problems,* and *social change.*

Conclusion

Although Ummites did apply aspects of the diagram-for-social-living to planet Earth, they did not use it in its totality. Their study focused on Earth's culture, complete with its *nonmaterial* (e.g., norms) and *material* (e.g., houses) components, but Ummites left out Earth's macro-level elements of social structure (e.g., social institutions). They only did a rudimentary study of Earth's culture. If the Ummites reported to their home planet what they found on Earth, they would either (1) falsely conclude the nature of social life on Earth; or (2) realize more expeditions were necessary to complete their study. How often are social scientists who study human cultures faced with these same alternatives?

Summary of Four Planets

Acart (Book #1); No-Name Planet (Abduction at Botucatu, Book #2); Iarga (Book #3); and UMMO (Book #4)

Table 3.1 identifies and describes each planet studied in chapter 3 of this book, along with identification of the date and place the incident occurred, and a description of the alien and its message to humans.

**Table 3.1: Description of Aliens and Planets
Acart, No-Named, Iarga, and Ummo**

Planet Descriptors	Plant Name			
	<u>Acart</u>	No Name/ <u>Botucatu</u>	<u>Iarga</u>	<u>Ummo</u>
Distance to Earth:	—	Located behind Earth's moon	Ten light-years	Fourteen light-years
Planet's geography	Continents; seas; very cold; beach; colorful	Arid desert; clean atmosphere	Pink-white ball with two halos; thick atmosphere and dim sunlight; heavy rains	Two-thirds water with many lakes and small mountains

Planet's demography	Twenty billion inhabitants	—	—	One race
First Incident— Place and Time	Sarandi, Brazil, May 14 to 23, 1958	Botucatu, Sao Paulo, Brazil, 1982	Off Netherlands coast, first published in 1969	Digne, France, March 28, 1950
Alien described	Pallid human-like	Humanoid with Japanese eyes	Humanoid with sea-faring bodies	Humanoid
Alien purpose/ meaning	Learn about humans; Instruction about use of solar; Future Earth colonization	Discuss earth's condition; Give contactee personal advice	Provide information to contactee about alien's planet	Learn about humans

As table 3.1 showed, two alien contacts took place in South America (both in Brazil) and two in Europe (i.e., off the Netherlands' coast and in France). In all cases, human witnesses described the aliens as "humanoid" or "human-looking." Also, in all cases, the purpose for the aliens contacting humans was either for the aliens to give us information about themselves, or for the aliens to learn about humans.

Where were these planets? Iarga and Ummo were trillions of miles away. The no-name planet was behind Earth's moon. Acart's distance was unknown.

Each planet's geography varied. One (Acart) had many continents, while another (Ummo) had only one. One (Acart) was very cold, while another (no-name planet) was an arid desert. One (no-name planet) had a clear atmosphere, while another (Iarga) could not see its own moon because of the dense atmosphere. Not only was there geographical diversity among these planets, there was also diversity within a single planet. For instance, the Arcartian planet was very cold, but it had a beach area where many Acartians recreated outdoors. Finally, two of these planets identified overpopulation as a reason for exploration of the universe and looking for places to live, such as Earth. For instance, Acart had twenty billion inhabitants, and Iarga claimed overpopulation to be a significant problem. The Acartian alien claimed they had come to Earth to explore it for potential settlement after we humans had exterminated ourselves by means of nuclear war.

4

NEAR-DEATH EXPERIENCES (NDEs)

Introduction

People have many questions about NDEs. This book addresses three of them:

1. What is an NDE?
2. What are the elements of an NDE?
3. How does the NDE treat God?

[AUTHOR'S NOTE: The words within quotation marks found in chapter 4 indicate passages taken from databank sources.]

What Is an NDE?

Dr. Raymond Moody is the father of the NDE field in the United States. He did not clearly define the NDE in his seminal book, *Life After Life*. He simply stated that it was a time *near* death. More recently, however, Dr. Pim van Lommel defined this phenomenon. "A near–death experience (NDE) is the (reported) recollection of all the impressions gained during a special state of consciousness, which includes some specific elements, such as witnessing a tunnel, a light, a panoramic life review, deceased persons, or one's own resuscitation."[1]

Dr. Lommel cited Bruce Greyson's NDE definition as: "Near-death experiences are profound psychological events with transcendental and mystical elements, typically occurring to individuals close to death or in situations of intense physical or emotional danger."[2]

Finally, Lommel offered a third definition from Janice Holden of the International Association of Near-Death Studies (IANDS): "Near-death experiences are the reported memories of extreme psychological experiences with frequent 'paranormal,' transcendental, and mystical elements, which occur during a special state of consciousness arising during a period of real or imminent physical, psychological, emotional, or spiritual death, and these experiences are followed by common aftereffects."[3]

According to these definitions, it is not necessary for a person to be dying to have an NDE. This factor raised some issues about what people called the phenomenon in the first place. If one does not have to be dying, why call it a "near-*death* experience"?! Perhaps a better label would be an *intensely stress-related experience* (ISRE).[4]

According to NDE literature, however, the NDE was a process that started at the moment death (or so-called death) began. At this point, the individual felt a sense of calmness, and, soon after, he or she exhibited an out-of-body experience (OBE). The person then returned to the body, after traveling through a tunnel into light, meeting people from the other side, and having a life review.

What Are the elements of an NDE?

According to many NDE researchers, most notably Dr. Raymond Moody, fifteen components constitute an NDE:[5]

1. The *ineffability* of the experience (or, the inability to put the experience into words).
2. *Hearing the news of one's own death.*
3. Having *feelings of peace and quiet.*

4. Hearing the *noise*; sometimes pleasant and sometimes unpleasant.
5. Having the sensation of being pulled through a *dark tunnel*.
6. Having an *out-of-body experience* (OBE).
7. *Meeting and communicating with deceased people,* usually relatives.
8. Seeing a brilliant *light* or a *being of light.*
9. Having a *life review* (a review of one's life).
10. Perception of a *border*; cross it, and never come back.
11. *Coming back,* and returning to the body.
12. Overcoming inhibitions and *telling others* about the NDE.
13. The experience has *effects on the lives* of experiencers (i.e., helps NDErs perceive/understand the future course of their lives).
14. Create *new views on death*; no longer fear it.
15. *Corroboration* of the experience.

How Commonly Do Dying People Experience These Characteristics?

I conducted a review of 2,259 NDE cases found in the Near Death Experience Research Foundation (NDERF).[6] I then extracted every eighth entry, creating a sample of 333 cases. The sample size has a precision level of approximately +/- 5 percentage points.

The sample drew information on seven of Dr. Moody's fifteen NDE elements:

1. A separation from one's body (#6)
2. Experiencing a tunnel (#5)
3. Seeing a light or light being (#8)
4. Meeting deceased people (#7)
5. Having a life review (#9)
6. Visiting an unearthly place (#10)
7. Perceiving one's future (#13)

In the pages that follow, we will examine each of these seven elements in detail, from the sociological perspective.

A Separation from One's Body (Moody's #6)

Table 4.1: Separation from One's Body—
OBE (Moody's #6) (n = 333)

Body Separation/ Had OBE	Body Separation/ No OBE	Experiencer Uncertain	Not Reported	Other
212	46	52	22	4
(63.7%)	(13.8%)	(15.6%)	(6.6%)	(1.2%)[7]

Table 4.1 summarizes the frequency with which NDErs[8] separated from their bodies during an NDE. One does not know the experience of those claiming *uncertain*. Nor is it known what happened to nearly 7 percent who *did not report* a finding. Clearly, a majority (64 percent) in the sample experienced the first significant element of an NDE because they had OBEs. Approximately 14 percent said they did not have OBEs.

Experiencing a Tunnel (Moody's #5)

After leaving their bodies, individuals passed through a tunnel, toward a light. How many in the sample went through such a passageway?

Table 4.2: Going through a Tunnel (Moody's #5) (n = 333)

Went through Tunnel	Did Not Go through Tunnel	Experiencer Uncertain	Not Reported	Other
109	135	39	45	4
(32.7%)	(40.5%)	(11.7%)	(13.5%)	(1.2%)

Table 4.2 shows that only 33 percent of the sample went through a tunnel. In fact, more did *not* go through it than did (41 percent versus 33 percent). I interpreted this statistic in a couple of ways. First, people did not progress far enough into the NDE to reach the tunnel. Second, they had an NDE, but this element was not part of it.

Seeing a Light or Light Being (Moody's #8)

How many people saw a light or light being?

Table 4.3: Seeing a Light or a Being of Light (Moody's #8) (n = 333)

Saw Light	Did Not See Light	Was Not Sure	Not Reported	Other
192	81	26	31	3
(57.7%)	(24.3%)	(7.8%)	(9.3%)	(.9%)

In the sample of 33 cases in table 4.3, 192 people reported that they saw a light. By far, more than twice as many saw a light than did not. There seems to be a discrepancy. Why did so many more people saw a light than go through a tunnel? See table 4.4 for a comparison between "tunnel goers" and "light seekers."

Table 4.4: Tunnel and Light Comparison (n = 333)

Tunnel and Light		Tunnel and Light		Tunnel and Light		Tunnel and Light		
Yes	Yes	Yes	No	No	No	No	Yes	Other[9]
92		7		53		68		113
(27.6%)		(2.1%)		(15.9%)		(20.4%)		(33.9%)

As many as 28 percent of those who went through a tunnel saw a light; only 2 percent did not. Of those who did not go through a tunnel, however, 20 percent still saw a light. Moreover, 31 percent who were uncertain, or did not report a tunnel, still saw a light. Clearly, passing through a tunnel is *not* a prerequisite for seeing a light.

Table 4.5: Saw a Light and . . .

. . . went through tunnel:	92	(27.6%)
. . . did not go through tunnel:	68	(20.4%)

. . . uncertain or did not report going through
tunnel: <u>35</u>   (31.0%)
                                                    Total: 195

As table 4.5 showed, in 195 of the 333 sample cases, NDErs saw a
light. This represented 58.6 percent of the cases. This complemented
the earlier statistic in table 4.3 that stated 57.7 percent of the total
sample cases saw a light. These statistics are only slightly different. I
concluded that approximately six out of ten NDErs saw a light, even if
they did not go through a tunnel, or were not sure they did.

Meeting Deceased People (Moody's #7)

How many NDErs met someone on their afterlife journey? Whom did
they meet? Did they know the person? Did these otherworldly beings
say anything? Table 4.6 identifies otherworldly beings (OWBs).

Table 4.6: Meeting OWB

Characteristic of Meeting:		# Involved
# of NDErs who DID meet an OWB:		172
# of Beings met:		
unspecified #	= 84	
1 OWB	= 67	
2 OWB	= 17	
3 OWB	= 12	
4 OWB	= 2	
5 OWB	= 2	
10, 12, 13 OWB	= 1 each	
# of NDErs who did NOT meet an OWB:		92

How Many OWBs Were There?

Out of the 333 sample cases, 172 NDErs met someone from the other
side. This represented 52 percent of the people who had an NDE.

NDErs met how many OWBs? For a vast majority of cases (49 percent), the answers were indeterminate. For as much as 39 percent of the time, an NDEr met one being. What did these statistics show?

Most people are petrified of dying. The idea that this is truly the end, and the fear of going alone on this journey, haunts many people. However, I discovered from sample cases that the journey to the other side for a (slight) majority of people is a *social*, not a *solitary*, event. Many NDErs were in the company of scores of others (OWBs). One can be assured of this point when only 28 percent of the cases emphatically expressed that they did not make contact with an OWB. In the remaining cases, NDErs were either "uncertain" or "did not report" making such a connection.

The nature of interaction between OWBs and NDErs is informative. From the perspective of OWBs, they might have seen each other as a group because they understood they shared an important common experience. NDErs had brief contact with them and could not judge the extent of involvement among these creatures. From the viewpoint of NDErs, OWBs might be a category, not a group. That is, merely beings that "glowed" but did not have a "personal" relationship with one another.

Finally, humans are not the only inhabitants of the other side. Animals resided there too! In one case, an NDEr saw her dog; in another case, an NDEr saw a black horse.

Who Was Seen?

Whom did NDErs meet on the other side of life? Did they know them?

In most cases (sixty-eight), it was a primary group member. Many saw a family member. Frequently, NDErs saw friends and significant others. Only one NDEr mentioned a secondary group member, an office mate.

They saw extended family members, such as grandparents, more often than nuclear family members, such as spouses, parents, and siblings. They witnessed grandfathers (seventeen) slightly more often than grandmothers (eleven). Do not be surprised by this statistic.

Women live longer than men, so there are probably more grandfathers on the other side than grandmothers.[10]

Parents were the most frequently seen members of the nuclear family. NDErs saw mothers (seven) and fathers (eight) virtually at the same rate. Among siblings, they saw brothers (four) more often than sisters (one). NDErs observed daughters (two), sons (one), husbands (one), and wives (one) least often. In one case, a mother saw her *future* daughter and son! In several cases, individuals observed uncles or other relatives.

Although these figures are not likely to hold up to scientific scrutiny, they give people a suggestion as to how it might be on the other side. Further research is necessary to solidify these numbers. Speculation, however, is possible. It is doubtful that most people know the demographics of those who die most often on Earth. Nor are the dying conscious of these statistics in the middle of an NDE! The groups that die at greater numbers on Earth are older people and men. Furthermore, the groups most often seen on the other side by NDErs were elderly and men. Can we conclude that NDErs were accurate in their observations?

What Did OWBs Say or Do?

There were ninety-four instances where OWBs spoke to, or sometimes did something with, an NDEr. In most of the cases (twenty-three), the NDErs heard a voice or voices, but the content of what the voice(s) said was unclear. The most frequent communications were a call to come over to the other side (ten), a directive to go back to one's life (fourteen), or a choice to do either (six). When OWBs called individuals to come over to the other side, they said "it was all right," and the NDErs felt very peaceful upon hearing this. When the beings told them to go back, they stated it was not the NDEr's time yet. They said the NDEr had to complete his or her work on Earth. In one case, an NDEr heard there was a mistake.

OWBs usually conveyed something positive. For instance, they stated "they were guardians who watch over, care for, and never leave us, and not to be afraid."[11] Sometimes there was an action taken. For example, OWBs showed landscapes, kids and grandparents playing together, or "ballet dancers swirling and surrounding." In one case, however, the creatures were "scary, screamed, and threw blood around."

There were occasions when an OWB directed an NDEr, for instance, "to move along faster in the tunnel" or "to go back." The overriding statement, however, was that NDErs had a choice; they were free to choose either to cross over and enter into the other world, or to go back to this world. In many cases, though, OWBs encouraged NDErs to go back to Earth in order to finish their mission/purpose (i.e., life's work). These OWBs functioned as socializing agents, in the sense that they directed NDErs (socializees) how to live/die. As socializing agents, these OWBs most often employed positive sanctions in the form of verbal encouragement. To urge compliance, often NDErs received life reviews to demonstrate to them the work they still needed to do before leaving this world.

Having a Life Review (Moody's #9)

How many NDErs had a review of their life while on their NDE journey?

**Table 4.7: Numbers of NDErs Who
Had a Life Review (n = 330)**

Had a Life Review	Did Not Have Life Review	No Report	Uncertain
71 (21.%%)	176 (53.3%)	61 (18.5%)	22 (6.7%)

As shown here in table 4.7, where one out of five NDErs had a life review on their journey to the other side, more than half did not. Although a life review is a popular topic in NDE literature, why did so few individuals in the sample experience a life review? Although sampling error might account for these statistics, it may also simply be that NDErs in the sample did not get that far into the experience.

How Does the Life Review Work?

What does the life review contain? What do people learn from their life reviews?

One can think of the life-review phase of the NDE in three parts: *medium, matter,* and *message.* The *medium* is the way in which the life review works; the *matter* is the content or particular subject matter of a life review; the *message* is the meaning conveyed by the life review.

The Medium of Life Review

As a medium, many NDErs described the life review as a *movie* or *filmstrip* that they watched, a *book* that they read, or a *photo album* that they looked through. This medium occurred very quickly, and life events were *not* in sequential order from early childhood until the time of "death." Rather, the life review was more like snapshots or a nonsequential film/video of life events. An NDEr could "hit pause," as it were, in order to focus on the details of a specific situation, or "hit replay" in order to go over a particular event.

In other words, these individuals experienced the effects of their actions upon others. If an NDEr hurt or loved someone, the NDEr understood how that person felt in response to the NDEr's actions.

The Matter of a Life Review

What was the content of these life reviews? It was "everything said or done by the NDEr that affected other people." NDErs observed some recurring scenes; however, most of their life reviews reflected experiences unique to their individual lives. For instance, one NDEr saw his brother's funeral and experienced it as though it were happening at that moment. Another NDEr saw his grandfather and experienced him as the judge of his life. One NDEr thought about his parents, and another saw his dad, who had died three years prior.

Most saw scenes from childhood and/or their whole life. "Nothing was hidden" and the "mundane and the important" both appeared in the life reviews of most NDErs. Most saw the "good and the bad" in their lives: their "addictive behaviors," their "higher (but yet-to-be-developed) selves," and the "hurts" they caused others to feel. In terms of time, one NDEr saw himself from the "moment of his creation," another saw herself up until the time of her "marriage," and a third saw "the recaptures (of) hundreds of physical lifetimes she had enjoyed, and life between these physical lives."

The Message of a Life Review
"Live and love; do not fear death or dying, and know there's a God who wants us to believe in Him." These were the messages NDErs learned in their life reviews. Most of the messages, however, concerned people's relationships. Overwhelmingly, OWBs told NDErs to "learn how to love."

Clearly, the love spoken of in life reviews spanned from personal to social. OWBs directed NDErs to love those close to them, such as spouses, families, and friends. They also told these individuals to "learn that we are all the same and need to obtain equality" and "that we need to stop putting people into categories, because they are walls that create hostility and bloodshed." OWBs told people it was "all about unconditional love" and that one's "task on Earth is to learn all aspects of love." One NDEr felt she "needed to assist others." Some NDErs aspired to "forgive," to "understand," to "act honestly," and "to take risks."

It was as if OWB guides, during the life-review phase of the NDE, were like psychologists. They directed the NDErs to take care of themselves, in an apparent effort to guide them to "get it right" so that they could love others. They told NDErs they were "acceptable," "their own judges," and that their "thoughts, feelings, and actions were all important." The OWBs encouraged individuals to "get on with it," telling them things like "life is fleeting" and "[you] need to complete the task—to help someone."

One of the largest obstacles most NDErs in the sample faced in regard to love was the fear of dying/death. Many of these NDErs were preoccupied with the end of life, and so they turned this fear—and the preoccupation that masked the fear—inward. Consequently, they became depressed and unhappy, sometimes even fearing other people. All these ingredients combined to inhibit these NDErs' ability to extend themselves to others. As an antidote to these inhibitors, life-review guides (OWBs) gave NDErs "prescriptions": "do not fear death"; "fear is an obstacle"; and so on. One NDEr learned, "I'm my own worst enemy, and I need to forgive myself." Other NDErs heard the message, "love those who are close to you, and forgive and recognize your mistakes."

Through the life review, NDErs discovered that they each were in a position to extend themselves to others once they had fixed themselves. Having recognized the need to accomplish such self-healing, NDErs next received the real message of the life review, which was the Golden Rule: "Do unto others as you would have them do unto you." In other words, the message was not about *me*; it was about *us*. Love was the element necessary to sustain the social bond among people. This was fundamentally a sociological message. In most NDEs, individuals learned about the interconnection among all elements of existence. "The universe was one enormous web, and a disruption in one part of it affected a disturbance in another part." A vast system of interacting parts connects everything. It seems as though the structure and functioning of the universe, as a system, puts sociology as a main framework for understanding the nature of everything!

NDErs learned that life on Earth was a "schoolroom to better ourselves." As one NDEr said, "We're here because life is like a school, and we learn to interact with each other; we're here to learn how to love." NDErs heard that people "have choices," and that they must "take responsibility for bad actions." They learned that there were consequences for the actions individuals took toward other people, and also for the thoughts they had about others. As one NDEr said, "[I] learned one's actions ripple through the lives of others. We send out waves of anger/hatred [and] you feel the response as ripples through [the] lives of everyone [you] touched." Another NDEr stated, "There are layers to the universe—we do something, and the universe shifts." Although there were consequences to actions, NDErs said they felt neither judged nor condemned during the life review.[12] The process is about learning and healing, not about judgment, condemnation, or punishment.

Visiting an Unearthly Place (Moody's #10)[13]

How many people near death saw a place on the other side?

Table 4.8: NDErs Viewing a Place on the Other Side (n = 333)

YES	NO	UNCERTAIN	NO REPORT
119	107	35	72
(35.7%)	(32.1%)	(10.5%)	(21.6%)

Table 4.8 shows there were quite a few NDErs who saw a place on the other side, but many did not. Those who were uncertain did see *something*. What did both of these groups see? One can categorize their reports into two groups: *ephemeral* and *specific places*.

> *Ephemeral Places*
> Ephemeral places had vague definitions in the descriptions given by NDErs. Simply stated, these were places where there were no concrete items to see or touch. NDErs described these amorphous places as "drawn into the universal, the cosmic vastness" and "outside of this universe." For some, such places were

simply described as "the light." For instance, NDErs said they were "in the light," or "in a higher level of atmosphere in another dimension in the light." For some, the light had color. One NDEr said it was "an infinite universe of purple [that] went on forever." Another claimed it was "an orange glow, like an aura, in which he floated." For two NDErs it was a "black void." For some, the void was *not* a cold and empty space; it was "a void in space that was warm and peaceful," according to one NDEr.

Specific Places

Specific places had concrete items, such as pathways, rivers, and meadows. Some NDErs described specific places in less detail than other NDErs did. Examples of general descriptions included "a door opened to the beautiful place with beautiful music"; "a sea of clouds and a bath of fire"; and "a region of light and a green field." A good many accounts of places on the other side, however, had more detail than the foregoing general descriptions.

Geographically, other worldly places ranged from the country to the city. There were landscapes that were park-/country-like gardens, meadows, woods, clay ground, deserts, and mountains. Populating these terrains were olive and palm trees, flowers (such as dandelions), and rabbits. Some of the verdant places had pools of water that were sometimes deep, as well as rivers, waterfalls, and oceans. Some NDErs saw clouds above them. Not all other worldly places were bucolic; some of them were cities. In one account, an NDEr identified the Cities of the Lord, Zion, and Commerce, while another claimed to have seen the Crystal City of Light. Another saw a "ball-playing field outside a city," while still another "saw a city from above which looked like a HO-scale train set below."

From a sociological point of view, other worldly places ranged from Gemeinschaft to Gesellschaft forms of social organization.[14] That is, some other worldly places were homey communities located in bucolic settings, while others were in large urban centers. How are we to explain such drastic differences? Are we to conclude that there were numerous other worlds, or were there different places within one other world? There was not enough information to draw a conclusion.

What Is This Place Called "Heaven"?

NDErs specifically named heaven in only seven cases. In one instance, someone described heaven as a "nice place as viewed from the outside." Another said she "glimpsed the pure joy of heaven." Still another gave more detail, "It was a landscape with clay ground, blue sky, tepid wind, and an olive tree; time and atmosphere were delightful." Finally, some saw heaven "with no sun or moon, no gravity or air . . . it had mountains that were beautiful, breathtaking, and sculptured on each side of the river."

What Was the Color of the Other World?

The other side seemed extremely beautiful. For many NDErs, it was a very colorful place. They mentioned the colors gold and green most often. There were golden gates, railings, and landscapes, and there was lots of green grass, green valleys, and an emerald stone. People saw other colors. Among them were blue, purple, and orange. Finally, there were neutral colors. There were "clouds in black or gray and white," a "white room," and "eternal blackness." All was not dark and gloomy on the other side, however, because NDErs also described a "shining garden" and a "bright light." They encountered a "bright light around themselves, and other worldly beings [OWBs]," and one simply said she "felt wonderful light."

How Does One Cross the Boundary to the Other Side?

When one entered the other world, he or she crossed a boundary. One said it was "cloaked in darkness," while another simply claimed it was "special." One said it was "a road." Often, NDErs spoke of another world as though there was only one. There were several accounts, however, that identified more than one place. Some spoke of heaven, purgatory and/or limbo, and hell, while others spoke of different "levels" or "planes." According to these accounts, not all was good on the other side! For instance, in one NDEr's case, "there were seven planes of existence; on one, souls [were] sexually tortured, [and] all vile forms but [he] could see the light above." Finally, the other world may not be in another place! One NDEr said, "[it] felt like touching the walls of my mother's womb before being born; no weight; everything soft."

Perceiving One's Future (Moody's #13)

How many NDErs saw the future? A little more than one out of five (22.2 percent) said that they saw the future. However, nearly half (49.5 percent) of NDErs in the sample did not see the future. The remaining 28.2 percent were either uncertain, did not report, or left this question unanswered.

In about one-third of the cases, NDErs identified a vague future. For instance, some said that they "could predict" and that "they knew everything." Others made claims about the future that anyone could make, such as "I'm not sure, but when I meet someone I get a feeling" and "I'm uncertain, [but] something is put into his head, and [then it] happens." Others claimed they had premonitions, vivid dreams, and strong intuitions. In one case, an NDEr claimed predictions about her family were "75 percent accurate, while everything else was 60 percent accurate."

Although the bulk of predictions were about the private lives of NDErs, many had visions of world events. One woman predicted "the fall of the Berlin Wall and a tornado in her hometown." Another said that he "sense[s] before [it] happens, like Guatemala and terrorist bombings in Bali." Finally, an NDEr "saw a meteorite fall into [the] ocean near Australia, [and the] entire continent disappeared into [the] ocean. In 2448, [the] Earth will have a temperature of 298°F, [and] people will be living in caves, [these] caves will be discovered, and they'll have strong fluorescent light[s]."

NDErs made more general world predictions. In one case, an NDEr said, "pride and money is [sic] the god of the Earth; [a] person [is] to give 90 percent to the Lord, and 10 percent to [the] individual." Another claimed, "Christ came to fulfill [the] Letter of [the] Law, and now it's the Spirit of the Law." Two other NDErs apparently received information about how the universe operated. For one, it was "If enough of the right people share in the belief of the given event, future events will happen."

On the personal level, NDErs had visions about their families' relationships and premonitions about their personal lives; NDErs also received counsel regarding their personal conduct. As one NDEr said, "[I] knew [I] had family troubles and needed to get a job to pay for my mom's divorce so she'd not be beaten by my dad." Another claimed, "[I] saw my unborn son." Still another NDEr said, "[I] foresaw Mother's and friends' deaths."

Other statements about their personal lives included such things as: "[I] could live [until] thirty-seven or seventy-three, and this was ten years more than [my] *past* life." "I'd not have a serious injury [and] would get out of Viet Nam [sic]." "Angels were guiding the doctors for me not to die." "If [I] went back, [I]'d suffer pain physically [and] mentally by [my] husband and others." "[When I] hear [the] song 'American Pie,' a name pops into [my] head, [and] then forty-eight to seventy-two hours later, that person dies."

Finally, NDErs gained insight into the conduct of their personal lives. For instance, "[I] had the need to be less stubborn, to give more, and to be more obedient and less of a bother." "[I] knew I had to go back to help someone who'd do some awe-inspiring things that would shift the universe to a nonchaotic order." "[I] needed to go back and try harder to be the best I could be and to help others and to spread the word of God."

In sum, what is the depiction of an NDEr? According to Dr. van Lommel, "there is no such thing as a classic near-death experience or a classic way of dealing with it."[15] The portrait of the typical NDEr in the sample, however, was he or she[16] had an *out-of-body experience* (OBE) (64 percent), did **not** go through a *passageway* or *tunnel* (41 percent), saw a *light* (58 percent), met *otherworldly beings* (OWBs)

(52 percent), did **not** have a *life review* (53 percent), visited another *worldly place* (36 percent), but did **not** see her *future* (50 percent). If one describes only those traits depicted by 50 percent of the NDErs, they are: he or she had an *out-of-body experience* (OBE) and saw a *light*.

How Can the People, Their Message, and the Place on the Other Side of Life Be Described?

In an effort to probe more deeply into the world on the other side of death, I examined data from other sources. There are four NDE organizations of note in the United States. Each one of them presents accounts of NDEs:

1. Near Death Experience Research Foundation (NDERF) www.nderf.org
2. After Death Communication Research Foundation (ADCRF) www.adcrf.org
3. Out of Body Experience Research Foundation (OBERF) www.oberf.org
4. International Association for Near-Death Studies (IANDS) www.iands.org

NDERF studies every element of the NDE, while ADCRF collects data on communications with entities on the other side of life. OBERF studies the out-of-body experience (OBE), as well as other aspects of consciousness that are not an NDE.[17] IANDS gathers general descriptions of the NDE without categorizing them as reported by Dr. Raymond Moody's classification schema.[18]

I could have used these four sources as databases for research. The OBERF and IANDS sites were *not* used for different reasons. Because this book focused on a sociological description of the world after death and of the people who populate that afterlife, I did not employ OBERF. This organization provided information about only one NDE element; that is, OBEs. I did not select IANDS data because of the great length of case descriptions.

At the beginning of chapter 4, I presented elements of an NDE. This presentation analyzed NDE cases that came from the NDERF database. This database yielded information about the people, places, and messages on the other side of life. I sought a more robust description of these three elements in order to provide a richer understanding. ADCRF data met this objective.

There were 1,274 cases[19] listed in the ADCRF website. I randomly selected 432 of these for a sample.[20] In that sample I found reports of people who communicated with beings (and animals) on the other side of life. From these reports, I abstracted the following:

1. The age, sex, and any other social factors of people on the other side of life.
2. A description of the physical place on the other side of life.
3. Identification of what OWBs said to people on Earth.

The addition of these database elements enriched the information I had about the people, places, and messages coming from the other side of life.

Who Are the People on the Other Side of Life?

What are their social characteristics (i.e., age, sex, and race)? What was the relationship of a witness to an OWB, if any?

The database did not present too much information concerning the social characteristics of the people on life's other side. Interestingly, males accounted for approximately one-fifth (21 percent) of the witnesses to an OWB, but they constituted a majority (52 percent) of the OWBs. Females accounted for slightly more than three-quarters (76 percent) of the witnesses to an OWB, but they represented only a little more than one-third (37 percent) of beings found on the other side. Surprisingly, there was more female NDErs than female OWBs.

Data reported OWBs as "young and vital." In most cases, this was the direct opposite of the way they appeared at the time of their demise. For instance, one witness said that his father died when he was eighty-nine years old, but when he saw his father in the afterlife, he appeared to be in his forties. In another case, a woman stated that her dad died at sixty-eight years of age, but when she saw him in the afterlife, he looked as if he were nineteen or twenty years old.

Witnesses also saw animals on the other side of life. Of the 432 cases in the sample, fourteen witnesses identified seeing an animal. Most of the animals they observed were cats and dogs.

In sum, the relationship that witnesses had with OWBs stretched from primary groups, such as immediate and extended family members or friends, to secondary groups, such as coworkers. The number of spouses seen on the other side of life was thirty-seven in total: husbands (twenty-nine) and wives (eight). The group most frequently seen on the other side of life was a nuclear family consisting of a parent or parents and their children.[21] For instance, of the 469 OWBs in the sample, 228 (48.6 percent) of them were members of a nuclear family: fathers (eighty-seven), mothers (seventy-five), sons (thirty), daughters (eleven), brothers (seventeen), stepbrothers (one), and sisters (seven). An extended family consists of the nuclear family plus other relatives, such as grandparents.[22] Adding grandmothers (thirty-seven) and grandfathers (twenty-six) to the nuclear family, the number of family members seen on the other side of life increased to a total of 291 (62 percent of cases). The combination of married couples and nuclear and extended families comprised 70 percent (329 out of 469) of the cases. NDErs also observed other relatives, such as aunts (ten) and uncles (eight), and, to far lesser extent, mothers-in-law (one), fathers-in-law (one), and brothers-in-law (one). Surely, meeting someone in the afterlife was a family affair!

For our purposes, a *significant other* is an individual who significantly influences someone else.[23] As might be expected, witnesses encountered a number of significant others, such as boyfriends (six), girlfriends or ex-girlfriends (five), best friends (three), good friend (one), first love (two), sweetheart (one), soul mate (one), fiancé(e)s (one), and significant others (as stated by the witness) (thirteen).

Individuals encountered secondary-group members far less often than primary-group members. For instance, people saw only four coworkers and one neighbor. There were also individuals who had very limited relationships, if any at all, with the people they saw. For example, NDErs viewed strangers fourteen times. Witnesses saw nondescript individuals, such as "a woman" and "people." People saw OBEs too. They saw angels (four), guides (one), ghosts (one), and God (one). Surprisingly, one person saw an extraterrestrial gray being.

Clearly, when someone saw an OWB in the next life, it was someone the witness knew. In most cases, this OWB was a close or distant family member, such as a mother, father, or relative. Social scientists claim that the family is the foundation that establishes human life on Earth. Apparently, the same may be true for the other side of life!

What Does the Other Side of Life Look Like?

Of the 432 cases reviewed in the ADCRF databank, 146 did *not* have any information that described the other side of life. That meant approximately one-third (33.8 percent) of the sample lacked any information from which to draw a picture of the world on the other side. However, 286 had some description of the afterlife. Of these, there were two types of afterlife descriptions: (1) *actual contact* with a being from the other side, and (2) witness *dreams* of the afterlife. The following section separates these two types. Is the actual account somehow different from the dream version?

Actual Contact with a Being from the Afterlife

Witnesses who made contact with the other world or OWBs had two different kinds of experiences. For the most part, the encounter with OWBs was on Earth, usually in the home of a witness. On some occasions, however, witnesses were on the way to the other world, had a glimpse of it, or were actually there.

What does the other side of life look like? Many religions have advanced the proposition that an afterlife has spirits or nonmaterial entities. Consequently, the other side of life need *not* be a physical space, because nonmaterial beings inhabit it. Nevertheless, most

NDErs describe the afterlife in physical terms. These are some examples: "tropical beaches," "animals grazing in pleasant areas," and "a beautiful place [where] flowers were huge." In one account, however, a witness "was walking, passing through a small nonquaint [sic] village that looked bleak and isolated." From sample cases, one might surmise the other side of life looked like a scene from *Little House on the Prairie*. Moreover, one gets the sense that this place on the other side had a pristine atmosphere, as the light there was always "vivid" or "bright." Seemingly, there was no pollution on the other side of life.

Regardless of whether it was an earthly witness or OWB who reported on the other side, it was an overwhelming experience for the describer.[24] One deceased entity simply said, "This is wonderful." Another claimed, "There are just no words to describe it." Still another OWB stated, "Can you believe this? If you could only see what I see now . . . I'm so happy." When a human witness left her body and proceeded to the next world, she saw "a place [that] was beautiful, flowers were huge; light was so bright and vivid."[25]

Shifting attention from the other world's *physical* environment to its *social* context, I noted it possessed culture as on Earth. There were material items (e.g., books and music) and nonmaterial ones, such as values[26] and norms[27] embedded in afterlife descriptions. Values constitute a foundation upon which norms rest. Once a group clarified what was worthwhile behavior for its members, it constructed norms or rules to reflect and protect these values. For instance, if a group valued "rugged individualism," it was likely to expect its members to work for the goods and services they wanted and needed. The group did not expect its larger community to provide these items to an individual.

Being sick and old was *not* a value in the afterlife. There seemed to be intolerance for these earthly frailties. Witnesses claimed OWBs were "half their age" (as compared to the time of their death). Also, OWBs were vigorously healthy, as opposed to the sickly and frail states of their health at the time of their deaths. For instance, a witness described her elderly grandmother as "transformed from a sick patient into a beautiful, younger woman." Another witness described her deceased grandmother, grandfather, and aunt as follows, "all three were young and incredibly beautiful, in their late twenties to thirties."

Furthermore, sample cases espoused three F values: *fun, faith,* and *freedom*. In one case, a deceased grandmother told her granddaughter, "[I'm] fine, having fun," and the witness heard her grandmother's friends laughing in the background. Another witness saw an old woman pushing against a barrier. She could not get through, and it frustrated her. Surprisingly, it was the human witness who gave direction to the OWB: "She (OWB) had to believe she could get through it (barrier), and suddenly a beam of light showed down, and she rose up." Finally, a deceased mother told her daughter, "Don't worry about me. Where I am, there's complete freedom, freedom, freedom!"

Additionally, a focus on *us,* not *me,* seemed to be a recurring theme in case after case. Witnesses learned that loving others in *this* world, in the *other* world, as well as *in between* these worlds, was important. For instance, after her experience coming in touch with the dead, one NDEr "wants to do good [sic] on Earth and to help others." In another case, a mother heard her dead daughter speak in her head, "Mama, God is love, and anything that you do that is not done in love is invalid." Love existed *between* "this" world and the "other" world. Surely, love is a universal value. It forms a foundation for the social bond among people on Earth, in the afterlife, as well as in between these worlds.

The Lord's Prayer proclaims, "thy will be done on Earth as it is in heaven," and I found this dictum in sample cases. Norms (or rules) distinguished between *appropriate* and *inappropriate* in both worlds. For instance, an OWB made contact with a witness, stating, "she broke the rules . . . and if she was caught she'd be punished." Negative sanctions punished norm-breakers, but the OWB did not specify a penalty.

Four rules appeared in the case studies. (1) A rule governed making contact with those on the other side (i.e., if humans contacted OWBs, they would answer; but there was a warning: "If you got in touch with them (OWBs), be prepared to hear things you may not want to hear"). (2) The living who did *not* want to stay on the other side could return to Earth; the border or boundary was there for a reason; cross it, and one would never get back. (3) The soul was described as a Rubik's Cube. "Each side was a section of the soul, and in each section there was a learning experience that needed to be completed to fill that aspect of the soul. An individual had to return to a section if h/she [sic] had not completed the learning experience in it. Once the puzzle of the soul was complete, one's whole spirit would remain intact with all the knowledge it collected. It would not have to return to a vessel (e.g., Earth) and would live in the presence of God forever."[28] The rule was that a section of a soul had to be completed before it could move forward. (4) People must finish their life on Earth before proceeding to the next. For instance, in one case, the witness could not die because "she had to take care of her unborn child." While in another case, a witness's deceased grandmother told her, "Go back down, my girl. You must continue your life . . . Go on. It's not your time."

Undoubtedly, there were other rules governing OWBs, but the above-mentioned rules were the only ones found in sample cases. From them, I concluded that life on Earth must be completed before journeying into the next life. How did people know their lives were over? They finished the section of the soul that was their cause while on Earth. If they arrived at the gate of death prematurely, the OWBs discouraged them from crossing over. OWBs directed them back to finish what they had to do on Earth. Also, people could get in touch with those on the other side of life. The beings warned them, however, that they may not like things they hear.

There were only a few references to material items of culture in accounts of the afterlife. In one account, the deceased paternal uncles of a witness were each seen holding a children's book. In another account, a witness "heard a roar and saw vehicles." Apparently, there were buildings on the other side too, as one witness reported she "suddenly appeared in a room . . . her grandfather was smoking a cigar." Another saw a baby boy on a blanket, and a witness saw her mother wearing a pink sweater.

The *Dream* Description of the Afterlife

In the ADCRF sample cases, there were approximately eighty-three references to dreams or to a witness being asleep. The predominant physical feature of the other side that witnesses saw in their dreams was "a beautiful place with a brilliant light, where surroundings were awe-inspiring [and] everything was perfect." Within this ideal environment there were "fluffy white clouds," "a large tree . . . with large branches," and a "rainbow." The physical environment of the afterlife was clearly a country scene. Some of the images witnesses reported were: "a meadow, with sun shining more brightly than ever" and "a beautiful garden built on various levels of steppes [sic] about nine feet high." There was "no weather; it's never hot or cold; no night or day," and it had "no time."

The following statement captured the essence of most witnesses' observations: "a lovely garden, a light-gray pebble path; light was intense and very bright but pleasant; colors were indescribable—green grass, blue sky, flowers much more beautiful and alive than on Earth." In one instance, though, an individual spoke of a harsh and colder place, identifying a wooden ship that was "icebound," and he was "running very fast up an icy tunnel."

Most cases described bucolic landscapes, but there were urban references. For instance, in one case, a witness was "walking along Main Street," while another found that she was "on the grounds of a huge, white, windowless building." Another witness saw her dad "in a hall of a building."

In a handful of cases, this paradise-like place had animals too. One witness dreamed of dogs, while another had a vision of her deceased "golden retriever." Another witness saw and heard "birds singing songs."

The demography of OWBs was sparse in case accounts. Witnesses saw OWBs ninety-six times in afterlife dreams. Of these, three-quarters were identified as males (forty-one), and thirty-one were females. These males and females are listed below, in descending order of frequency of occurrence:

Males:		Females:	
1. Dads	17	1. Moms and	9
2. Grandfathers	5	Grandmothers	9
3. Man	5	2. Sisters	3
4. Husband	4	3. Aunts and Women	2
5. Son	3	4. Wife, Daughter,	
6. Brother	2	Girlfriend, Great-	
7. Boyfriend	2	Aunt, Female, She	(1 of each)
8. Uncle	1		
9. Stepfather	1		
10. Him	1		

Identified men were black, short and dark, and young. There were eight accounts where the sex of the OWB could be either male or female. Most were friends (three), while each of the following had merely one case cited: grandparents, soul mates, patients, monks, and guides. There were only three cases of other worldly entities mentioned. One was a fellow deceased entity, and the other was two angels.

The nuclear family of mother/wife, father/husband, and their dependent children (including brothers and sisters) accounted for 43 percent of the citations. The extended family (consisting of a nuclear family plus other family relatives [e.g., aunts and uncles and grandfathers]) comprised 61 percent of the listings. Once again, I noted that relations with OWBs definitely constituted a family affair! There was only one case of a secondary-group member identified, and this was a "patient." Only one significant other was mentioned, and it was a "soul mate." Strangers were in heavy evidence in this very small sample of OWBs. Witnesses identified such strangers (twelve times) as "people," a "figure," and a "vague entity."

Cultural material items, such as clothing, appeared in roughly sixteen cases. There were two types of attire mentioned: (1) clothing worn by a person before their death; and (2) apparel received in the afterlife. Earthly clothing included such items as "a baseball cap and his favorite shirt" and "long-sleeved khaki shirt, pants, and soft suede-like work boots." Afterlife clothing was always white, and the witnesses described it as "pure white" (i.e., "beaded white dresses" and "white robes.")

There were varieties of housing styles described, such as a "Greek open air stadium," "the interior of a log cabin," "a bungalow," and "a huge, white, windowless building" (mentioned previously). Individuals noted other objects, such as a "wooden ship" (mentioned previously) and "telephones."

On the nonmaterial side of culture, one witness said, "nothing bad was there." Some afterlife beings, however, did mention less-than-perfect relations there. For instance, a witness's departed mother could not "come near her or be made aware of the witness's presence." OWBs gave no reason for this norm. In another case, when a witness asked her deceased sister why she could not leave, she said, "the males said she [I] can't." I drew two points from this statement. First, apparently, there were rules in the afterlife, as the deceased could not leave for some reason. There was sex dominance in the afterlife. Apparently, women's liberation had yet not arrived there!

Sample cases showed OWBs from *their* point of view. For instance, they did not think of themselves as "dead," but, rather, as "transformed." As one deceased person put it, "I'm not dead. I just don't have a body." When describing herself to the witness, a deceased sister said, "She was there, and she still existed." From their viewpoint, where are they? One OWB said it was "heaven," while a deceased grandmother said that she "didn't call it heaven." In another case, a witness learned "the invisible live among us and contact us." Apparently, the deceased inhabit (1) heaven; (2) somewhere "out there" that is not heaven; and (3) on Earth, moving invisibly among living people.

There were only three times when witnesses noted the physical form of OWBs. One witness described an OWB as "solid," while in another case, the OWB "had no substance, and his hand passed right through the phone." These beings, however, were an active lot. In one case, a witness observed an OWB being "busy with a variety of things," while another OWB attended a "sporting event in a stadium."

What were the purposes of these activities? One was recreational. The other "was given work to do that she liked so she could concentrate on adjusting to her crossing over." Consequently, the passage from this world to the next can challenge some of the dying.

Finally, a witness learned that her dead boyfriend "was getting to know a guy from Arkansas." As revealed in the case, her boyfriend *was* the fellow from Arkansas, and the purpose of his activity was "to get reacquainted with himself, and the life he had on Earth."

Most after-death communication cases were among family members whose postdeath relationships either remained the same or changed somehow. For example, in one case, a deceased dad told his daughter that he "was always with them; [and would] wait for as long as it takes." While in another situation, the "father-daughter relationship seemed to disappear; [it] seemed like someone she knew very close." Moreover, these loving relationships existed not only between the living and the dead but also among the dead. For example, one deceased person said, "[it was] a beautiful place where everyone loves [me]." Finally, according to this deceased person, love moves into the future "and [we] will be together in other lives."

As to the difference between "actual" and "dream" accounts, *no* discernible dissimilarity existed between them. In both types of accounts, the other world was a bucolic place populated with the witnesses' deceased relatives, who were usually nuclear-family members. In both actual and dream renditions, the witnesses' views of the other world were indescribably beautiful. There were material objects, such as books and buildings, in both versions, and the deceased were young and healthy in both types of accounts.

What Did Other Worldly Beings (OWBs) Say to Humans?

Of the 432 cases,[29] 247 of them (57 percent) recorded an OWB communication[30] with a human witness. Consequently, a majority of contacts by OWBs with humans included a communication. OWBs seemed to be a loquacious crowd; that is, when it came to their interest in talking with humans! In a like manner, OWBs' effusiveness extended to how much was said in a single communication. Often it was more than one thing. For instance, in one case, an OWB commented on her loving relationship before her death, while also describing her dying process and a description of heaven. Although OWBs' communications were often verbal, they could also be telepathic, and, to a lesser extent, it was nonverbal through the use of gestures (e.g., smiling or waving good-bye).

Furthermore, these communications arrived in the form of a *dream* (37 percent) or a *direct contact* (64 percent).[31] Skeptics may be surprised that twice as many communications between OWBs and humans were *direct contact,* rather than through *dreams.* Nonbelievers may explain away the after death communication (ADC) as a human's imaginative dreams. It is hard to dismiss such an occurrence, however, when a human witness encounters a mist or fog in the bedroom, and that amorphous entity transforms into an image of his or her deceased parent. Finally, was the content of messages to humans different in these two forms? The following section distinguishes between these two types of OWBs' contacts with humans.

Direct Contact with a Human Witness by an OWB

There was often more than one message embedded in communications from OWBs. For instance, a departed husband told his wife: (1) he loved her; (2) someone murdered him; and (3) heaven was not a place, but, rather, a condition that existed wherever the soul was present. It was difficult to categorize this communication because of its many facets. Regardless, five themes occurred in the *direct* communication of OWBs with humans:

1. They sought to *prove* that they were present among humans. For instance, when one witness asked simply, "Is it you?" An OWB answered, "Yes."
2. OWBs were intent on commenting upon their *relationship* with humans. Most notably, they conveyed their *love* for humans in messages, such as a husband who committed suicide said to his wife, "I love you. I always have and always will ..." Also, OWBs apologized for their bad behavior while on Earth. For example, when a son died in a bad car accident, he said to his mom, "Momma, I'm sorry." They also reassured, supported,

or offered their protection to shore up witnesses' relationships with other humans. Finally, the departed discussed the status or quality of their relationships with specific humans when they (departed) were alive.

3. OWBs commented upon their *state of being.* For instance, one OWB simply said, "I'm all right." When asked why it took so long to return, another OWB said, "Because I can't come back all at one time." Another OWB blurted out, *"I am damn dead"* They did not seem too upset with their state of being. One of them claimed, "I am very, very happy, Valerie dear. You are *not* to worry. I am very, very happy."

4. They simply *communicated* making contact (e.g., "a ball of light which was her brother smiled at her and was so at peace, and it said, 'Fran Bod (his nickname for her) you're not going to throw up on me are you?'"). Sometimes they gave advice (e.g., "her grandmother spoke to her in her head and said, 'Don't tease the baby, Thao [sic]'") At other times, they said "hello" or "good-bye."

5. Finally, OWBs spoke about the *other world.* For instance, one OWB said, "Oh, Judy, you are going to love it here. It's so beautiful. Even the children don't cry when they fall down." A deceased dad said, "Don't be sad. This is wonderful."

Direct OWB contacts with humans demonstrated the sociological nature of this phenomenon. There was a true interaction[32] between humans and OWBs. OWBs most often wanted to communicate with humans. After they established their existence and presence among humans, OWBs sought to establish or continue a relationship with them. Clearly, death was not the end of a relationship with a deceased member. The relationship either continued into the next life as it was on Earth, or it transformed into something new. Sometimes the departed person moved on to other/new relationships in the afterlife.

Additionally, OWBs were polite as they greeted or concluded contact with humans. Cultural folkways continued into the next world, as OWBs and humans used social etiquette when they said "hello" and "good-bye" in their communications. OWBs displayed values and norms when they gave advice to humans. The pursuit of happiness and successful, loving relationships were examples of values promoted by OWBs.

An OWB Communicated through a *Dream* to a Human Being

Human dreams contained the same five previously noted themes of communication. Through their *dreams*, people saw how well or poorly their deceased person was doing, and they received glimpses of the other world. How individuals received communications about such items was *proof* that the deceased person still existed in an afterlife; or, the humans received *advice* about how to live their lives on Earth. For example, a husband told his wife that her mother spoke to him from the other side and said she was fine. All was not good, however, for the departed on the other side of life. For instance, a deceased father said to his daughter, "Get me out of here, Pat." Furthermore, Raymond Moody's characterization of the 'indescribability of the other world' was evident in human dreams. For instance, in one case, a daughter asked her departed father what happened to humans after they died and what they did in the afterlife. He responded, "Honey, I wish I could tell you, but I can't; and even if I could, you wouldn't understand it on your earthly plane." The vast majority of descriptions about the state of being of deceased people were positive. Most deceased persons said such things as "I'm happy and okay."

There was a social structure on the other side. I noted that a parallel existed between the social structure of this world and the other world. In two accounts, there was *stratification*. For instance, a grandfather told his granddaughter, "I'm higher up than she is; she's below me." (The "she" referred to the grandfather's wife; or the granddaughter's grandmother.) In another case, a departed individual told what she did in the other world: "We have responsibilities over others, [and] then there are others that have responsibilities over us."

What happened to people after they left this world and entered the next one? Witnesses received answers to this question in many dreams. First, sometimes the dying process was problematic. For instance, a guide from the other side told a woman that her mother "was given work to do that she liked and could concentrate on so she'd adjust to her crossing over" (as stated previously). Second, the part of a human that existed after life on Earth seemed a bit hard to grasp. A grandmother explained it quite succinctly: "Life and personality (soul) will exist beyond life." Third, there is a connection between this world and the other world. One deceased person said, "We're all connected, not just humanity but all of creation." Another said, "Yeah, the body I traveled through life [in] is gone, but that isn't me. I'm just [as] alive as you are. I'm just somewhere else."

Not all of the dreams focused on the other world and the process of getting there. Some of them concentrated on humans' time while on Earth. For instance, a departed mother praised her daughter when she said she was proud of her. In another case, a deceased person encouraged his daughter by saying, "I wanted to see you because I know you are going through a hard time, and I'm worried about you. ... Someday, when your life is finished there, this is where you'll be; this is what you're working for. I want you to go back, and I will see you again someday, but not until the time is right. You have a lot to do yet." In another case, a dead boyfriend apologized for fighting with his girlfriend. A father offered protection when he promised to watch over his son.

Themes found in *direct contacts* between OWBs and humans also appeared in humans' *dreams* of the other world and its inhabitants. The only difference was that there were more direct contacts than dreams in the ADCRF sample cases. Therefore, regardless of the medium through which afterlife (or after-death) beings communicated, the message was the same:

1. Love one another on Earth.
2. Life continued after death, albeit in a different form.
3. Love and health existed on the other side.
4. The other world was indescribably wonderful.
5. Deceased beings were active, and their life forms continued into future realms.

Additionally, these accounts painted a less-than-perfect picture about the afterlife than portrayed in the popular NDE literature. I noted that there was stratification and that males held dominant positions. Therefore, some similarities between here and there existed. Women sought equal rights through social movements on Earth for many decades. Perhaps this effort needs to be extended into the afterlife too!

What Were the Aftereffects of an NDE?

What were the effects of an NDE upon those who have had them? Did their lives change, and, if so, how?

There is a problem that arises in evaluating the aftereffects of an NDE. It lies in distinguishing between the changes that come out of the NDE itself from those that resided in the act of nearly dying. In his book, *Consciousness Beyond Life: The Science of the Near-Death Experience,* Dr. Pim van Lommel addressed this issue. Taking people who had experienced cardiac arrest, he compared those who had an NDE with those who did not. Also, he examined these groups two and eight years after they had their medical problem. He found that NDErs, after eight years, had higher scores in the following areas:[33]

1. Showing emotions
2. Less interest in others' opinions
3. Acceptance of and compassion for others
4. Involvement with family
5. Less appreciation of money and possessions
6. Increased awareness of the importance of nature and the environment
7. Less interest in a higher standard of living
8. Appreciation of ordinary things
9. Sense of social justice
10. Awareness of the inner meaning of life
11. Decline in church attendance
12. Increased interest in spirituality
13. Less fear of death and dying
14. Increased belief in life after death.

Dr. van Lommel concluded that the NDE fostered the above changes in cardiac survivors beyond their encounter with dying. I saw similar results in the sample used here. Some NDErs said, "[I] now show others love, and I am sorry for [my] wrongdoing"; "my relationships have changed; they are more respectful, considerate, and compassionate"; and "[I] love life more." Others said, "[I] don't worry about money and what others think"; "[I] appreciate my life, wife, and simple pleasures more"; "[I'm] not interested in organized religion"; "[I'm] not afraid of death"; and "[I] know there's life after death."

Although many cases in the sample agreed with those NDErs in Dr. van Lommel's study, others held different viewpoints. For instance, many claimed the NDE did not alter their personal and religious beliefs and practices. Their lives did not change. NDErs expressed a variety of ideas concerning religion. One NDEr said, "religions are man-made, [and I have] no love of man-made church rules." Another claimed, "[I] was liberal [but] now [I am] more [of a] conservative Christian." Still another asserted, "[I] continue to be a Catholic." Finally, almost without exception, those who believed that their NDE was real lost their fear of death and dying. Finally, for some NDErs, their marital relationships are heavily taxed. There is a high divorce rate among NDErs.[34]

What Is the Meaning of an NDE?

Did NDErs believe their encounter was something real? What did they learn from it? The overwhelming number of NDErs felt their experiences were "real" or "probably real." Most came to the understanding there *was* life after death. For them, death was not an end, but, rather, a transition. NDErs put it in these ways: "Life has no end; no beginning"; "Death is a passage"; "Death isn't the end of life. It is an existence that is different from this one and a whole world better."

How Does the NDE Treat God?

What about God?

In the United States, polls showed 92 percent of Americans believe in God.[35] Seventy-nine NDErs mentioned God/Jesus/Lord/Source/Creator. Only nineteen actually saw or experienced him or her.[36] One NDEr said, "There is just dark and [there is] no God." Many more claimed that they no longer *believed* in God. They *knew* that he or she exists. One NDEr claimed, "[I] know there's a God." Another affirmed, "I spoke to God. He exists."

How Is God Described?

Many theologians say God is indescribable, and one NDEr said, "People asked me to describe God, and I reply, 'Imagine an aardvark running across a stage and people writing down their descriptions of it—all [of them would be] different and difficult to understand.'" Finally, NDErs described God in these terms: "He is love," and "[God is] our energy source who [sic] needs us, and we need Him."

Where Is God? Where Does God Live?

For many, God resided in heaven, which was a place beyond Earth. One NDEr had a more metaphysical understanding. He said that he "sees reality is only a 'veil' covering another 'veil'; pulling [sic] them aside and see deeper into what can only be called the name God—what can never [be] known or comprehended but can be more aware of our being—a part which is never apart." For others, God is not that far. "God is alive and [He is] inside of me." And for another, "the church of God is in our soul, and not in a creed or in a building."

Although God materialized to some NDErs, this was a rare event. The solemnity and vastness of this deity made it difficult for NDErs to describe him or her. For many, God resided in heaven. For others, this divine being was beyond humanity's comprehension. Finally, some thought God's presence lived within all living entities.

PART III
WHAT'S IT ALL ABOUT?

5

WHAT ARE WE TO CONCLUDE ABOUT UFOS, ALIENS, AND NDES?

The preceding chapters have taken us on a journey into space and time. We have traveled to "other places" on planets well beyond Earth, and into a time after all of our tomorrows. We have documented the social worlds of other planets, as well as the society in the afterlife. What did we see during these observations?

Other Worlds in Space, UFOs, and Aliens

I posed and answered five essential questions about UFOs and aliens:

1. *Who* were the aliens that came to Earth? *Who* were the humans that saw them? Were there social characteristics, such as age, sex, and race, that described aliens and the humans who saw them?
2. *What* were UFOs? *What* were their characteristics?
3. *When* were UFOs and aliens seen? Did these observations happen in specific years, months, and hours?
4. *Where* were aliens and UFOs seen? Were they seen only in certain places on Earth, or were they seen everywhere?
5. *Why* did they come? Did aliens have messages for humans?

What Were the Social Characteristics of Aliens and of the Humans Who Saw Them?

I reviewed 1,656 cases drawn from two samples in 2011 and 2012. From among all of them, 412 cases contained sufficient information to describe what aliens looked like. This represented slightly less than 25 percent of the cases. The following summarizes the physical attributes of aliens, as described in chapters 2 and 3 of this book.

- height
- sex
- race
- physical characteristics (e.g., body shape and eyes)

In addition to physical traits, I also cited aliens' movements and sounds, as well as some material elements of their culture, such as their clothing color and accessories.

A typical alien in the samples ranged in height from two inches to thirteen feet, two inches in the first sample, to thirty-one inches to nine feet in the second sample. Clearly, aliens were a diverse lot. Some were so small a human could step on them inadvertently, just as they might accidentally step on a hamster. Others were so frighteningly tall that they resembled a man on stilts. A typical alien, however, was approximately five feet tall, while a human is between five and six feet tall. In terms of height, then, a typical alien was similar to an average human.

Interestingly, the literature recorded only two alien sexes. The universe is an enormous place, and it is conceivable that more than Earth's two sexes would be found in it. This was not the case. There were only males and females throughout the cosmos. Furthermore, they possessed the same sex characteristics (e.g., reproductive organs, female breasts, and male hairiness) as on Earth.

It was difficult to determine the sex of aliens. This was because of their distance from human observers, or because their clothing camouflaged their sexual identity. Most of them, however, appeared to be males. Occasionally, a female crew member accompanied a male counterpart, rendering cosmic travel a predominantly male activity.

Both humans and aliens recognized different races among their populations. In the case of aliens, races spanned from light to dark. On one end of the spectrum, aliens were white and pale; on the other end, they were reddish-orange, blue, green, and black. However, in 58 percent of cases, aliens were gray or white.

I've also recorded alien body parts in previous chapters. Their overall body shape varied widely. For instance, aliens were described as "humanoid," "resembled an octopus," "holographic," and "reptilian." Some were thin, some were heavyset, and some were muscular. One witness said an alien looked like the "Michelin Man."

The data only infrequently identified alien eyes. When mentioned, witnesses described alien eyes in terms of their size, shape, and color. Alien eyes were large, slanted, or round. They glowed in fiercely red, yellow, or black. Witnesses usually saw two eyes, but one alien had "a cyclops eye that floated to the ground." Finally, their eyes were likened to those of cows, cats, and fish.

Reports often cited alien heads, which were large and egg- or pear-shaped. Some alien heads had protrusions coming from them. Most alien heads had hair that was long or cropped, and wavy, mousy, or fuzzy. Alien hair color varied from blond to black, just as human hair color does. Reports did not mention alien arms much. When cited, they were described as "long and skinny, and jerking around mechanically." Arms had hands, fingers, claws, or wrists at the end. Hands were either "human-looking" or "pincer-/claw-like," and they had from three to eight fingers.

The creatures' mouths were often small and motionless. A "slit" was a popular description for the alien mouth. Presumably, mouths ingested food, as aliens often communicated telepathically. Covered with clothing, alien legs, knees, ankles, feet, and toes received little mention in the databank. When seen, legs were "small" and "stringy," and two in number. Aliens' movements were often "herky-jerky" or "mechanical." They moved "slowly," "took huge leaps in slow motion," or were "stiff-legged [in a] bouncy fashion."

Alien noses were not often seen. When observed, witnesses described them as "small" or with "two slits." Ears were "long" and "floppy," or aliens had "antennae on the sides of their heads." People saw aliens "walking or floating" more often than they observed them making sounds. Aliens moved quickly and slowly, and their walking motion was mechanical or stiff-legged. They fixed their spacecraft, collected water, and carried devices, such as boxes. Sometimes their actions threatened humans. For instance, when an alien touched a human's arm, he burned it. Alien sounds included "sizzles" and "clicking noises."

What items did aliens have in their culture? They had bland-colored clothing that was mostly "silver," "white," "blue," or "black." Their clothing consisted mostly of "suits," "coverall/overalls," or "uniforms." Some people thought that aliens were crew members because they wore uniforms, or they thought that aliens were workers because they wore coveralls. Often, aliens had accessories, such as "square" or "translucent" helmets and "gloves," "belts," and "hoods." Finally, these beings had weapons, such as a "laser gun" and a ".357 mm pistol." All these material items protected the aliens on their journeys to distant planets (e.g., Earth), giving them the means of assessing what they found.

Flipping our analysis from aliens to humans, we found most witnesses were between ten and nineteen years old, with approximately 66 percent under the age of thirty. Most were males. Witnesses spanned a broad spectrum of occupations, from professional to unskilled workers.

What Were UFOs' Characteristics?

Most people understand that a disc-shaped object flying in the sky, or settled on the ground, is a UFO. In its broadest sense, however, a UFO is *any* unidentified flying object. For instance, "lights" and "balls of energy" fall into this category. Most disc-shaped UFOs, however, ranged in size from thirty-four to thirty-seven feet long, thirty-four to thirty-seven feet wide, and six and a half feet tall. Some were much larger. For example, one was "ten times the size of a plane," while another was "half the size of the moon."

Although witnesses saw a disc-shaped UFO most often, they also noted other shapes, such as a "cigar" and a "boomerang." Regardless of shape, most UFOs were "metallic" and often "silvery" in color. Some UFOs, however, were "orange," "red," "green," and "white." Most UFOs had one predominant color, but they could be two-toned. For instance, some were "very bright, with a dark underside." They also changed colors, perhaps indicating an alteration in speed or direction. This color transformation may have occurred upon landing, or as camouflage for a hostile or unknown environment.

The lights on UFOs served different functions. Occasionally, witnesses reported "bluish" or "white" interior lights. Also, UFOs had warning lights similar to those on airplanes. Colored lights, usually in the form of a beam, emanated from the craft. The lights transported aliens in and out of their vehicles. Finally, sometimes the lights hid aliens from hostile humans, immobilized aggressors, or effected memory loss in humans. At times, witnesses saw lights, but their origin was not a UFO. It was "balls of light" on or near the ground.

UFOs were marvels of maneuverability. They hovered, stopped in the sky or just above the ground, or jutted upward and downward at great or slow speeds. Occasionally, humans heard "hissing sounds like a million snakes" or a "dull roaring sound." Some UFOs traveled at incredibly high speeds, such as thirty-nine thousand miles per hour, while others were observed "stopping dead in the sky."

Finally, the UFO characteristics indicated technology far in excess of anything human-made. They flew great distances and engaged in maneuvers that literally ran circles around humankind's most-advanced aircraft. These material items of culture demonstrated that alien societies were in the advanced stages of development.

What Years, Months, and Hours Were UFOs and Aliens Seen?

Sightings occurred mostly during a twenty-year period between the 1950s and 1970s. Since the late 1980s, the numbers have fallen.[1] Most sightings happened during the months July (197), August (174), and October (192), and the fewest were in January (112), February (112), April (111), and May (102). The majority of recorded sightings occurred in North America and Europe during the summer and fall seasons. These seasons saw more people outdoors.

Sightings occurred most frequently during nighttime (9:00 p.m. to 12:00 a.m. [midnight]), and least often during daytime (6:00 a.m. to 3:00 p.m.). I accounted for this pattern by noting that most northern hemisphere people are at home in the evening and at work during the day, thus making it easier—and harder—to view UFOs in these places at those times.

Where in the World Were Aliens and UFOs Seen?

The two countries with the most sightings were the United States and France, respectively. Although virtually every country on Earth reported sightings, the predominance of them was in North America (54 percent) and in Europe (27 percent). Thus, four out of five sightings worldwide happened in these regions. Why? It may *not* be a result of more UFOs. It may be a function of the frequency of reporting them. The United States and Europe have a plethora of UFO organizations set up for collecting these types of data, more so than other places on Earth.

Within the United States, California (seventy) had the most sightings, and Ohio (fifty-five) and Texas (forty-three) had the second and third most, respectively. Two of these were among the five most populous American states (i.e., California and Texas). This is not surprising, as more people present a possibility of more sightings.

Why Did They Come? Did Aliens Have Messages for Humans?

How could beings from the other side of the cosmos communicate with earthlings? Usually aliens connected telepathically with humans, but sometimes they spoke "a mixture of Spanish and English" and "an unintelligible language with a digital musical quality." Aliens rarely (4 percent of cases) conversed with people, but when they did, they spoke about a narrow range of concerns. They gave commands (e.g., "sit down"), had requests (e.g., "asked for water"), delivered reassurances (e.g., "don't be afraid; nothing bad will happen to you"), or disseminated information (e.g., "I'm going to regenerate you by a procedure that is not yet known on your planet").

They traveled vast distances (e.g., 2.4 million light-years) from unknown planets (e.g., Clarion) to present practical, global, and individual messages to humans. For instance, aliens wanted water or titanium for an unidentified purpose. Also, they presented themselves as "emissaries of peace" to assist earthlings in search of world harmony. Finally, one alien said he came to "take possession of a witness's soul" while another came to "impregnate her."

Aliens implored earthlings to think and act on behalf of Earth and its people. It was as if they held a mirror up to humanity, showing how excessive use of power, engagement in nuclear wars, and ecological devastation would yield mass destruction of the planet. Recognizing humanity's free will, aliens never threatened to intervene into human decision making. They never threatened to invade or take over the planet. They did, however, warn humanity that they were ready to populate Earth when humans kill themselves off through war or ecological destruction. Aliens claimed life was precious and rare in the universe, and when they found it, they sought to protect it at all costs.

Human Opinion about UFOs and Life on Other Worlds

Public polls recorded people's openness to the UFO phenomenon. In the 1940s, 90 percent of the US population did *not* believe in UFOs.[2] Today, a majority are believers. Moreover, when asked if there was life beyond Earth, 80 percent of respondents thought that there was. More than a majority (54 percent) professed extraterrestrial life was intelligent, while almost two-thirds (64 percent) thought ETs contacted humans. Only 37 percent believed that aliens contacted the federal government, while 72 percent held the government concealed this contact.

The Social Structure of Alien Worlds

After describing UFOs, aliens, witnesses, and the public's opinion about these phenomena, I presented a more in-depth analysis of the social structure of alien worlds. In chapter 3, I used the sociological perspective to analyze four alien planets' societies: Acart, no-name planet (abduction at Botucatu), Iarga, and Ummo. Following a brief description of alien and human contact, I identified the ecology of each planet and described each planet's population. Also, I recorded each planet's culture, along with its system of stratification, institutions, social problems, and social change.

In table 5.1, I applied five sociological concepts (i.e., *culture, stratification, institutions, social problems,* and *social change*) to a description of the four planets covered in chapter 3. From this table, you will ascertain a description of the social structure of four other worlds.

Table 5.1: Sociological Components Applied to Planets Acart, No-name, Iarga, and Ummo

Name of Planets

	Acart	**No-Named (Botucatu Abduction)**	**Iarga**	**Ummo**
Sociological concepts				
Culture Nonmaterial Language	N/R	Pigeon-like cooing	Language of all living things	Double language; expressed two ideas at once
Status and role	Sex-role equality but prefeminist roles	N/R	Sex-role equality	Sex-role equality, but wives submitted to husbands
Values and beliefs	(1) Work; (2) noninterference; (3) competition and recreation; (4) equality; (5) compassion and peace; (6) knowledge; (7) efficiency	(1) Work and activity; (2) environment; (3) self-reliance	(1) Justice; (2) efficiency; (3) freedom; (4) love; belief in unselfishness for group survival.	(1) Modesty; (2) respect and love; (3) abstract and rational thinking

Norms	N/R	(1) Do not fear teachers; (2) do not wear self out before the trip home	N/R	(1) Body to be covered; (2) status based on an individual's aptitude; (3) copulation based on couples' psychobiological exam results
Culture, Material Components				
Spacecraft	Rounded; solar-powered; 100' diameters; like two bowls inverted on each other; opaque light; light beam	1,640' long; disc-shaped; orange, green and lilac; bell-shaped; light beam	50' diameters with 3' opening on the top; control panels inside; others had 90' diameters; polished silver with slots underneath; antigravity machine	43.5' diameters; three legs for landing; propelled by magnetism
Housing	Humanlike, with platforms outside for plane landings	Various color changing stones; without doors; like caves and isolated	Glass tanks in the form of ring 900'x300'; organized into rectangles	Tubular structures part above and below ground
Transportation	Motorized flying machines; no ground transportation; streets used by pedestrians	N/R	Extensive and efficient rail system	N/R
Technology	Solar-created magnetic-powered aircraft	Strange machine seen	Made to conserve natural resources; no moving parts	Communication capable of reaching intelligent species in other galaxies
Social stratification	First had stratification, but now no social classes	N/R	No Stratification	Stratification

Social institutions				
Marriage	Monogamy	N/R	N/R	Monogamy
Family	Nuclear	N/R	N/R	Nuclear
Economy	No money; take what you need	N/R	No money; few huge "trusts" produce foods/ services; no property ownership (it is loaned); competition but no inequality; no materialism or conspicuous consumption	No money; take what you need
Government	World government; council headed by "Son of the Sun"; had elections	N/R	N/R	Representative democracy with four leaders qualified by psychophysiological exams
Education	N/R	N/R	Basic to advanced; done in home building; teacher an observer; technology	N/R
Religion	Monotheism	N/R	Monotheism	Monotheism; scientific proof of soul's existence
Social Problems	(1) Overpopulation; (2) war; (3) poverty; (4) crime	N/R	Overpopulation	(1) Sexual practices (masturbation, prostitution, using contraception, and homosexuality); (2) torture

Social Change	War to no war; stratification to none	N/R	N/R	Government changed from monocratic to tyrannical to the appropriate use of scientific principles in governing

An examination of these four alien planets revealed they had societies that could be analyzed with sociological concepts. Thus, comparing and contrasting Earth's social structure with these four "other" worlds was possible.

Language was an essential ingredient for establishing relations among intelligent beings. Communication among sentient beings was impossible without communication. Grunts and groans go only so far conveying to others one's range of wants and needs for survival. Just as Earth had various languages so, too, did the rest of the universe. For instance, Iargans listened to vibrations from others but did not vocalize any sounds, while the no-name planet had a "pigeon-sounding tongue."

Every society had statuses and roles. Wherever one traveled in the universe, males and females held specific statuses and played particular roles. For example, on Acart, Iarga, and Ummo there was equality among sexes. However, the parts females played on Acart and Iarga were similar to those on Earth prefeminism. Equality existed in their workplaces, but at home, females raised children, made meals, and submitted to their husbands. When females were supervisors in plants or on spacecraft, males had difficulty following their orders.

Alien and earthly cultures had the same components. That is aliens' ways of life included material objects, such as houses, factory buildings, and transportation systems, as well as nonmaterial elements, such as the values of love, efficiency, and work.

Every alien society had values. They guided societal members into behaviors deemed important for living there. Examples of values included work, efficiency, love, and equality. Overpopulation depleted environmental resources on many planets, so they valued efficiency.

It minimized environmental exhaustion, and things lasted forever. Societies encouraged members to take only what they needed, and conspicuous consumption was nearly a sin! Clearly, this is a far cry from how people in America conduct themselves. Consumption is not only tolerated, it is encouraged. In fact, two-thirds of the US economy operates on consumer demand. A whole industry (i.e., advertising) exists to convince people to buy goods and services, even if they do not need them. Simply, if the Joneses have it, everyone needs to get it!

On some planets, equality evolved over time. On Iarga, stratification created an undue amount of wealth and poverty. This inequality fueled an increase in crime. The have-nots took from the haves.

Another popular extraterrestrial value was love. However, love "out there" was not the same as love in modern, Western societies. For example, on Earth, love means physical and emotional appeal (at least in the West). It is the *zing* feeling one gets in the presence of one's beloved. On Ummo, however, couples united when their scores on psychobiological exams were compatible. Also, when they copulated, their screams came from affection or sentiment, not physical pleasure. Earthly women may be sex objects, but on Iarga, females received respect.

Another extraterrestrial value was the preservation of the environment. In fact, most messages from aliens indicated that they thought humanity was going to blow itself up in a nuclear war, and then kill the planet with radiation. They came to help humanity avoid this outcome, but would not interfere in humans' decision-making process. This was because they recognized humans' free will, and understood it was humanity's responsibility to solve its own problems. Aliens followed universal laws of noninterference. However, if humans did not save themselves, some aliens were ready to repopulate Earth with their own species.

Social institutions, such as marriage, family, economy, government, education, and religion were found on all or some of the four planets studied. Moreover, witnesses described some alien institutions as remarkably similar to those on Earth (that is, at the time the authors wrote these books). For instance, on Acart and Ummo, marriage systems were monogamous, and their family systems were nuclear. Females raised children and submitted to their husbands, but they worked outside of the home, unlike most human females on Earth in the 1950s.

Their economic systems were more communist/socialist than capitalist. This contrast paralleled the difference between socialist/communistic European economies, and the capitalistic economy in the United States in the twentieth century. Also, aliens seemed to provide for their consumers according to Karl Marx's adage, "From each according to his abilities, to each according to his needs."[3] Alien economic systems differed from their earthly counterparts, however. Alien worlds had no money, and aliens registered, borrowed, and/or returned goods. Consequently, there was no private ownership of property.

Alien governments evolved from nation-states on each planet to a world (planet-wide) government. When an alien planet was organized into individual countries, conflict extended to the point their inhabitants nearly exterminated themselves. Following this carnage, they decided to unite under one world (planet-wide) government. Although many leaders and citizens on Earth urged their nation-state governments to form a world government, there was only some movement toward that. For instance, the United Nations formed in 1945, and the European Union formed in 1999. Fundamental forces throughout the globe have pushed back efforts to unite Earth's people. Nation rights, more than world rights, seemed to be popular on our planet as of this writing.

When societies valued knowledge, they needed a system to deliver this "commodity" to their members. When these societies were very large, their delivery system was a complex organization. So it was on planet Iarga. The Iargans organized their educational system into classrooms found on the top of every housing complex throughout their society. Iargans' advanced technology enabled them to integrate this educational system. An electronic structure delivered lessons on large screens at each housing complex, and teachers functioned as observers aiding their pupils.

In a like manner, the contemporary US educational institution seems to be following the Iargan pattern. As Earth's population grows and society's technology advances, the educational system in America is evolving from traditional bricks-and-mortar form into distance education. In other words, colleges are delivering courses via the Internet more often than in face-to-face classroom instruction. The cost of higher education, rising gasoline prices, and a youthful population accustomed to using electronic devices drives this transformation.

One might think advanced, technological societies like the four planets studied might have abandoned religion, as they relied more on science. This was not the case. Planets Acart, Iarga, and Ummo not only practiced religion, but they were monotheistic. Coincidentally (or perhaps not), these planets' religions paralleled the monotheistic Roman Catholic religion of the earthly societies where aliens made contact. In Brazil, France, and the Netherlands, Roman Catholicism was the dominant religion. In fact, the Ummites claimed their religion was much like Christianity, and Iargans claimed, "[The] Resurrection itself will happen suddenly. The signal will be given by Jesus Christ." Moreover, although earthlings debate the existence of a soul, on Iarga a scientific principle *proved* its existence.

These planets were technologically and scientifically developed, and they had attained the advanced stages of societal integration. They did, though, have problems. Overpopulation, war, crime, and poverty were social problems faced by most of them. It was instructive to see how the planets handled these issues. Aliens understood that the consequences of stratification were crime and poverty. They knew that crime and poverty flourished when some members got more societal "goodies" (e.g., income, wealth, prestige) than others. When they realized this connection, the societies abandoned stratification and instituted equality. Acart and Iarga eliminated poverty, and Iarga substantially reduced crime.

Finally, when societies were as old as these, social change was inevitable. Every area of social life changed over time. As populations grew, the organization of their societies became more complex, and natural resources became taxed. Efficiency of operation became a necessity. For instance, Iargans constructed products, such as rail systems, to last forever. This would safeguard resources. Moreover, overpopulation fueled planets' space programs. Aliens explored the universe for potential places to move to once they ran out of space and resources on their own planets. Politically, when their nation-states warred, and nearly annihilated themselves, they formed one-world governments. Economically, they formed institutions and systems where their inhabitants received goods as they needed them. Aliens did not own property, societies did, and they loaned to individuals. Religiously, they integrated principles of spiritual beliefs into tenets of science. As a result, they *proved* the soul's existence, and they believed in one God who "generated" the universe (i.e., WOA on Ummo).

From a cultural absolutist's position,[4] these planets were in the advanced stages of development compared to Earth. For instance, all of them possessed technology that permitted them to travel trillions of miles. They communicated over these distances, often through telepathy. Although a world government and equality within societies were debatable goals on Earth, these planets accepted them as survival principles.

For such advanced people, though, some of their technology was primitive. They had leather upholstered chairs and steel drums on spacecraft, and they had stone caves for housing. Although aliens suspended restaurant tables from ceilings, the tables resembled those found in any restaurant on Earth in the 1950s or 1960s. Moreover, their mores were not very sophisticated. For instance, their attitude toward females seemed backward by contemporary earthly standards. Although females were equals at home, they held roles similar to those of Western women before the Women's Liberation Movement. For example, when Acort took Artur home, Acort's wife made the meals and took care of their children.

One gets a mixed picture from a study of these four planets. These aliens seem advanced in some ways and primitive in others. How can this discrepancy be explained? There are four possibilities: (1) These planets, in some ways, *were* technologically inferior to Earth's cultures. (2) Given that many witnesses did not have much education, they had limited vocabularies to describe what they saw. (3) In a general way, human witnesses had a limited vocabulary to describe ways of life so different from their own. (4) These were stories invented by human writers who were bound by and limited to the cultures from which they came.

Other Worlds in Time, NDEs

After examining "other worlds" in *space*, we investigated an "other world" in *time*. I researched two databanks for information about time after death: (1) Near Death Experience Research Foundation (NDERF), and (2) After Death Communication Research Foundation (ADCRF). There were 333 cases taken from NDERF and 432 cases from ADCRF. From these 765 cases, I identified points along the dying process, from the separation from one's body to returning to it. I assessed the experience's effect on the future lives of individual NDErs, and I also explored the meaning of an NDE itself.

I used the two above-mentioned databanks for NDE cases. In ADCRF, there was a distinction between *dreams* and *actual* incidents. There was no significant difference found, however, among witnesses' descriptions of what they saw on the other side of life.

Nearly two-thirds of NDErs separated from their bodies, but only one-third went through a tunnel. Next, NDErs saw a light or a light being. Nearly 58 percent of cases experienced this NDE element. As people went deeper into the NDE, they came in contact with deceased entities. A majority (52 percent) of NDErs got this far in the experience.

Whom Did They See?

ADCRF enlarged the understanding of who was on the other side. Most NDErs saw primary-group members, such as parents or marital partners. People most often saw a nuclear family, consisting of parents and children. They also encountered extended family members, such as grandparents, as well as "significant others," such as close friends.

NDErs rarely encountered secondary-group members, such as coworkers, on the other side of life.

An inverse relationship existed among the sexes both in this life and the next. Although there were more female than male witnesses on Earth, there were more males than females in the afterlife. Similarly, many of the deceased were old and riddled with disease when they arrived in the afterlife, but, when seen by witnesses, they appeared young and vital.

Sometimes afterlife entities had messages for NDErs. Most were directives to come over to the other side or to go back to Earth. OWBs projected feelings of compassion, love, peace, and security to NDErs. They told NDErs "not to be afraid" and reassured that "everything would be okay." Insofar as OWBs gave direction to NDErs, they functioned as *socializing agents*. They taught people how to behave in this world, as well as in the next.

Only 20 percent of NDErs had life reviews. The life review was described as a "filmstrip" of every incident in one's life. The review portrayed significant, insignificant, good, and bad incidents. Mostly, NDErs felt the emotions that they had caused others to feel. The life review directed NDErs to "get their lives in order" so that they could love others. Unconditional love was the most significant activity of life. It gave the most meaning to the existence on Earth, as well as throughout the universe.

Where Is the Afterlife and What Does It Look Like?

Sometimes NDErs provided vague descriptions of the afterlife, while others offered no description of it. Some located it in the "cosmic vastness," while others said it was "outside the universe." Some said they were "in the light," while others placed themselves "in a higher level of atmosphere in another dimension in the light." NDErs described the light as "purple," "orange," and "dark." Some identified specific objects in the afterlife, such as "beautiful clouds," "windows," "green fields," and "music." There were "landscaped parks," "countrysides," and "gardens." NDErs saw "mountains," "valleys," and "olive trees," as well as "blue sky" and "fluffy clouds." Not all descriptions were bucolic. Some depicted cities. In one account, an NDEr was "walking along Main Street," while another saw her dad in "a hall of a building." Finally, sometimes the afterlife received "heaven" as its nomenclature.

ADCRF cases identified the other side in *physical* terms. Its ecology included beaches, flowers, and animals. Individuals described the afterlife as a pristine place with vivid light. Mostly, it was simply a "wonderful" place.

Culture, values, and norms comprised the afterlife's *social* world. It valued health, not illness. If someone arrived in heaven in a decrepit state, he or she transformed into bountiful health. Other values included fun, faith, and freedom. A grandmother told her granddaughter she had fun in the afterlife. Another deceased person stated that she needed to believe in the (dying) process for it to continue in a successful manner. A third deceased person informed her daughter she had an abundance of freedom in the other world.

There were norms governing contact with those on the other side. If one made contact, he or she needed to be prepared to hear what the person on the other side would have to say. A rule directed earthlings to finish their life on Earth before proceeding to the next one. Also, if a witness wished to go back to Earth, he or she could. Finally, a norm described the soul as a Rubik's Cube that needed to be put together before progressing to other levels of being.

If one crossed a boundary, he or she would be dead. It was the point of no return. It seemed like a path or road. The afterlife, or heaven, was on the other side. People depicted the afterlife in various ways. In one case, a person said, "There were seven planes of existence; on one, souls were sexually tortured . . . but he could see the light above." Many NDErs who got this far into the experience did *not* want to return, because of the overwhelming beauty, peace, and love emanating from the light source.

Surprisingly, the deceased did not see themselves as dead. As one said, "I'm not dead. I just don't have a body." Not all of them thought they were in heaven. One claimed, "The invisible live among us and contact us." The deceased lived in a variety of afterlife places, such as "heaven," "someplace other than heaven," and "invisibly among people on Earth."

What Do the Deceased Do in the Afterlife?

The departed are very active on the other side. They worked, recreated, and sought to discover who they were. One witness viewed a deceased person "busy with a variety of things," while another appeared at a "sporting event in a stadium." A deceased boy examined his life on Earth when he claimed to a witness, "[I] was getting to know a guy from Arkansas" (the birthplace of the deceased).

In sum, love and health existed in an indescribably wonderful place where deceased beings remained active, and their life form continued into future realms.

Did the Deceased Communicate with NDErs?

The deceased did communicate with NDErs. In ADCRF cases, 57 percent of the deceased communicated with witnesses. This communication came through a dream, direct contact, or both. Most often, it occurred directly, and when it did, there were five themes:

1. The deceased sought to *prove* they were *present.*
2. They commented upon their *relationships* with humans.
3. They referenced their *state of being* in the afterlife.
4. They noted that they *communicated* with a human (or humans).
5. They *described* the *other world* that they inhabited.

Social interaction was a universal activity that penetrated time. The social bond among people while on Earth continued into the afterlife. It could be in the same form or a different form. Folkways guided interactions between humans and the deceased, as they greeted each other with "hello" and bid each other "good-bye." The deceased revealed their values and norms in their communication with humans. They informed people that their time was well spent when they pursued happiness and fostered loving relationships.

Although one departed person said that the other world was "pretty much like described in books," another agreed with Raymond Moody's claim that it was indescribable. The social structure of the other world is similar to structures on Earth. Stratification into higher and lower positions existed. Some had authority and responsibilities over others. It was unclear as to how they got their positions. Was it by merit or appointment? Men dominated women, as males held higher positions in heaven.

What Were the Aftereffects of an NDE on an Experiencer?

Only 22 percent of experiencers saw their future lives. Only one-third of them could describe vaguely what it would be. These individuals said that they "had a feeling" when something was going to happen, for instance. They had visions about personal and public events. For example, they foresaw family relationships and had premonitions of their personal (future) lives. One said he knew that "[I] had to get a job to free my mother from my abusive father."

NDErs' feelings, thoughts, and actions changed after an NDE. While vast numbers left organized religion to experience spirituality, others went back to the church. One felt "more isolated." Many "improved [their] social relationships," and also "improved communication with others." Others "appreciated life" and "did not fear death."

How Did NDErs Understand the Meaning of Their NDE?

Overwhelmingly, these individuals *knew* the NDE was real. They came to understand death as a transition into a better life, and not an end. Most NDErs *knew* God existed, while only a minority of them mentioned the deity in their accounts. Most experiencers focused on relationships. They noted the importance of love, getting over one's fear of death, and recognizing the afterlife as the most incredible place in the universe.

Summary

In conclusion, while sojourning as a sociologist, what did you learn from your trip to other planets and into the afterlife?

Clearly, intelligent beings, regardless of where they were in space or time, engaged in social interaction. It mattered not if they were here or there, or whether it was now or after this life. The norms governing the formation of groups, and, later, societies were the same. When groups grew large enough, they formed societies and created a culture. These societies had material things, such as clothing and housing, as well as nonmaterial items, such as values of equality and work. Societies developed norms to inform their members of appropriate and inappropriate behaviors: right versus wrong, and normal versus abnormal. For example, the no-name planet directed its members not to fear their teachers, while planet Ummo taught its members that it was appropriate to cover their bodies.

Regardless, if one met sentient beings in space or time, he or she would note that all such beings congregated and created social bonds among themselves. Truly, intelligent life in space and time was essentially social. People recognize the "me" generation in the United States. In the universe and in the afterlife, however, the pronoun *me* is less important than *we*.

Did a relationship exist between UFOs and NDEs? Was there a correspondence between space and time? Both questions speak of social relations; one was on the macro level of social living, and the other was on the micro level. UFOs and aliens spoke to the public level of social life, while NDEs expressed the private level. The extraterrestrial messages continually described how society could be structured, while the NDE literature explained how humans ought to relate personally with one another—that is, how to love one another.

Although we concluded the journey noting the social nature of life throughout the universe, questions remain. For example, why is death a path to a life after this one? Why does one's journey pass through pain and death? Why is the other world separate from this one? Why haven't aliens made themselves readily visible to all on Earth? Why do they wrap themselves in mystery? Why does consciousness exist?

Arguments for and against UFOs, aliens, and/or the afterlife are framed within the context of the scientific method. Recently, scientists expressed their doubts about the validity of this method as a way of knowing the nature of these other worlds (and life on Earth). Also, the human mind is finite, whereas these fields of inquiry seek explanations about seemingly infinite space and time. Perhaps answers will come to us in the future; perhaps not. There is no doubt, however, that the quest will continue.

6

A VIEW TO THE FUTURE

We are swimming in a sea of New Age, holistic, and spiritual awareness that seems to have flooded over the dams on old beliefs and constricted consciousness ... the evidence is everywhere that New Thought is becoming mainstream.[1]

The Social Construction of Reality

Throughout history, humans imagined life, as well as intelligent life among the stars. They have also wondered about and conceived of life after death. As time marched on, individual speculation on these matters evolved into group theories. These theories then continued through the generations until a point when people held them as ultimate truths. For instance, humans certainly saw pock marks on the moon from the first time they looked at that celestial body. Later, some thought those marks resembled a man's face. Surely, these observers shared their opinions, and, over time, the "man in the moon" became a cultural idiom (at least in the West). Today, no one believes there is a man in the moon, because people have looked at the moon through telescopes and astronauts have even visited the moon. Humans now consider it a "fact" that the "man in the moon" is merely the reflection of light and shadows that make this apparent configuration. Current knowledge explains the face as a *pareidolia*.[2] In short, science replaced the myth.

In terms of life after death, people (i.e., Egyptians) once believed their bodies needed to be intact after death so that their identity (soul) could enter the next life.[3] Today, religions propose a variety of options for the hereafter, such as an afterlife where the soul emigrates from the earthly plane to either heaven or hell, depending upon one's value while still alive (i.e., varieties of Christian religions). Advances in the physical and life sciences, especially in the medical profession, are changing contemporary ideas about death. For instance, Pim van Lommel, MD, has asserted that the increased incidence of NDEs is the result of advances in resuscitation techniques.[4]

Simply, its members' ideas and inventions (e.g., telescopes) that determine what a society sees out there. Their culture shapes not only *what* they see but also *how* they understand. Culture serves as a cauldron within which humans actually come to see things, as well as to understand and explain them. For instance, some allege Native Americans did not see the first ships arriving from Europe. They could not because they did not have words in their vocabulary to see them. It was a marginal person in their society (i.e., a medicine man) who had the "vision" necessary to see them. This individual then "enlightened" others in the society to "see" the ships too.

Culture is a medium created by humans, and it functions as a framework for seeing and understanding things. As this point applies to space, Steven Dick, quoting Otto Struve (1962), identified three great revolutions of the last four hundred years. These revolutions accounted for a change of perspective in humanity's understanding of the universe. The first was the Copernican Revolution. It moved the Earth from the center of the solar system. The second happened in the 1920s and 1930s, when scientists asserted that the solar system was not in the center of the Milky Way. The third was the revolution occurring now, which posits that "we are not alone in the universe."[5] What accounted for this shift in consciousness?

According to John J. Macionis, there are three sources of cultural change:[6] (1) *invention,* such as the telegraph or computer; (2) *discovery,* such as the New World of the Americas or ice on Europa (a Jupiter moon); and (3) *diffusion,* which is the spread of ideas or objects among cultures. For instance, Thomas Aquinas adopted Aristotle's Earth-centered idea. He claimed that God came only to Earth because it was unique. It was the only place in the universe with intelligent life; thus, its inhabitants were worthy of salvation.[7]

As Steven Dick[8] showed, at first, most believed there were dead rocks "out there," but speculation emerged about the possibility of life in outer space. In other words, thought shifted from seeing a *physical universe* (dead rocks) to understanding that there was a *biological universe* (life on other planets). This change in consciousness emerged from invention (e.g., telescopes and other powerful instruments), which led to discovery (e.g., Earth and the solar system were not in the center of the universe). These ideas then diffused throughout the world, and thereby influenced the thinking of numerous scientists in a multitude of fields, from the physical sciences to the social sciences and humanities.[9]

According to Dick, these three revolutions indicated a move from a closed, geocentric view of the world to a vision of an infinite universe. The closed world, which had only an earthbound understanding of humanity's place in the universe, evolved to a perspective of seeing humans within the context of an infinite universe.

Dick's observations illustrate what sociologists refer to as the "social construction of reality." Thus, a group constructs what humans understand is real. Simply, reality is a social construct. In *The Social Construction of Reality: A Treatise in the Sociology of Knowledge,* Peter Berger and Thomas Luckmann state that their book concerns "the relationship between human thought and the social context within which it arises."[10]

According to Berger and Luckmann, knowledge and reality itself are understood within a social context. If a society is folklike and rural where people are "personal," that society will use different imagery to describe space and time than a mass, urban, "impersonal" society will use. Thus, a Gemeinschaft-type American society of the 1600s offered a different description of outer space and the afterlife from a Gesellschaft-type[11] society in the 2000s (or beyond).

As societies change from one type into another, everything within them changes. For instance, examples of moral dicta may be put forward in stories about animals in Gemeinschaft-type societies. These same maxims may be found in stories about gangs living in urban environs in Gesellschaft-type societies. Living in a rural society, one may conceptualize answers to these issues in fables with bucolic themes. The Big Bad Wolf who terrorized the Three Little Pigs spoke to the threats perceived in an agrarian life. It directed people to prepare for such threats by building more secure physical structures. This same concern within a computer age may come in the form of a computer game where soldiers fight terrorists in the Middle East to make Americans safe at home.[12] Although the message is the same, its presentation will change as the society changes.

On the other hand, the message itself can also change. The messages to humans from aliens found in the 1950s UFO literature were that (1) Earth needed to eliminate nuclear arms, and (2) nations must seek peace. More recently, the message has been that humans must save the planet's environment. These themes reflect changes on Earth. That is, in the 1950s, the world was embroiled in a Cold War between the West and what was then the Soviet Union, transfixed by the threat of a thermonuclear World War III. Gradually, starting in the 1970s and even more so following the fall of the Soviet Union, the world engaged in "saving the environment"—a movement that persists to this day. Simply, the alien message changed from a warning about nuclear war to concern about environmental degradation. This change mirrored the alteration in human concerns, from nuclear war to environmental destruction.

Although the social construction of reality may be a persuasive explanation for what people see and understand, there are two problems with it:

1. Why do people all over the world report similar descriptions of UFOs?
2. Why do people everywhere and from all walks of life ask about and describe visions of an afterlife?

First, if what one sees and understands is relative to one's culture, how do we explain the consistency of descriptions across the globe? For example, from Brazil to the United States, people described UFOs as "inverted saucers." Doesn't this common observation prove that these objects are real? If people from different societies throughout the world describe UFOs in the same way, are they not real? Perhaps! These societies are similar in social structure, even though they exist around the planet. Therefore, what they see and how they describe it will be similar. For example, Gemeinschaft-type societies, such as those in Renaissance Europe, described UFOs as "fiery chariots,"[13] while those in Gesellschaft-type, Western twentieth-century societies described them as "technologically advanced metallic discs."[14]

Second, why are humans seeing objects in the sky, and why are they perceiving deceased people in an afterlife? Furthermore, why have they seen these things for millennia? Doesn't the fact of seeing these things for virtually all of time indicate that they are real? Perhaps! Another consideration is that one sees these things because they "speak to" the perennial questions of humans. There are fundamental yearnings of the human heart. These longings extend through the ages, from prehistoric times to modern days. People want their lives to be worthwhile and mean something. They want to know what is out there and what happens to them after they die. Although these are perennial human longings, the ways in which people conceive, understand, and express these longings does vary. Each society contemplates these ideas in its own fashion.

Paradigm Shifts[15]

Fields of knowledge see their paradigms shift. Most notably, as it applies to our purpose, in this book we have noticed a change of models explaining the great "out there," as well as elucidating what happens to humans after death. For instance, Steven Dick demonstrated that considering the possibility of life on other worlds became part of Greek culture in the fifth century BCE. According to Dick, Epicurus argued that an infinite number of other worlds existed beyond human senses, but not beyond human reasoning.[16] The ancient Greeks reasoned that there were an infinite amount of atoms, but all of them could not be contained in a finite, earthly realm.[17] In the fourth century BCE, Aristotle argued the Earth was the center of the universe. It was unique. A plurality of worlds with the Earth at its center then took hold of the Greek psyche.

However, the West's worldview shifted from a plurality of worlds to perceiving a singular one. Thomas Aquinas (AD 1225–1274), a significant figure of the powerful Roman Catholic Church in Europe, took Aristotle's cosmology and shaped it into a Christian framework. He imagined that God's son, Jesus, lived, died, and resurrected in the only place where intelligent life existed: namely, Earth. Further, Aquinas stated that intelligent beings (or humans) were the only ones who would be made in God's image. Thus, the people of this time understood the Earth to be the center of the universe, and the only place where intelligent life could be found. Why else would God send "his only begotten son" if it were not the center of the universe, and the only place where there was intelligent life?

Enter Copernicus . . .

Copernicus displaced the Earth from its central location in the solar system, and, with that displacement, humankind became dislodged from its central locality. Copernicus did not postulate there was life on other planets, but he gave the theoretical underpinnings necessary to imagine other habitable planets.[18] Also, astronomy adopted the Darwinian worldview of evolution from biology. If organisms on Earth evolved, then planets, stars, and, indeed, the cosmos itself evolved too. Worldviews were changing from anthropocentrist to cosmologic. The Earth's centrality in the universe, and humans' uniqueness within it, shifted to the noncentrality of the Earth and humans' nonuniqueness in it. Other worlds with intelligent life became a real possibility.

The Greek and Copernican plurality of worlds' viewpoint conflicted with the Christian understanding of the singularity of the Earth, and of the uniqueness of humans. Thus, we have an outline of the evolution of human thought as it applies to an understanding of the great unknown, detailed below.

Ancient Greece	Medieval Europe	Twentieth-Century World
Epicurus: An infinite amount of atoms not able to be held on a finite earth; therefore, there a plurality of worlds exists.	*Copernicus:* The Earth and humans are not in a central position.	A plurality of worlds exists; Earth and humans are not central.
Aristotle: The Earth is the center of universe; therefore, the Earth is unique.	*Aquinas:* The Earth and humans are central; there is not a plurality of worlds, but a singularity (i.e., only the Earth).	

This change of worldviews, or paradigm shifts, opened the twentieth-century mind to the possibility of life and intelligent life on other planets. As Steven Dick indicated, there was a revolution of the mind, a transformation that sought confirmation.[19] The twentieth-century mind was set for seeing intelligent life "out there." Public opinion polls measured the extent of this shift of consciousness. As stated previously, in the 1940s, 90 percent of Americans did *not* believe in UFOs.[20] However, an NBC poll in 2012 suggested that 77 percent of Americans think that there is evidence that aliens have already visited Earth.[21]

A paradigm shift occurred regarding views on the afterlife. In the United States, the NDE field began in earnest in the 1970s. Prior to that, most people avoided the topic of death, not to mention life *after* death. Many local hospitals did not even discuss the topic of death/dying. In fact, one hospital's procedure was for staff to transport any dead body on the lowest gurney shelf, with the corpse covered so no one would know there was a deceased person on the gurney. According to Raymond Moody, prior to 1975, medical personnel referred to afterlife visions as a "Lazarus Syndrome." They considered any such experience to be a medical malady caused by hallucinations or mental illness.[22]

After Moody, individuals understood the NDE as a fact of dying. The paradigm shifted from understanding death apparitions as religious visions or mental aberrations to realizing that these "visions" were a real part of the end-of-life stage. Simply stated, those close to death experienced the NDE as a "normal" and natural part of the dying process.

The medium used to normalize this phenomenon was the *scientific method*. First, researchers identified and studied hundreds, and now thousands, of cases. Scientists collected, analyzed, and reported data from the nearly dead. This brought about what Bruce Greyson called "Dr. Moody's whole new world" and "a change in our collective worldview."[23] Now people recognize an NDE as a legitimate phenomenon, and they studied it as a scientific matter. The NDE came into this world from the spiritual realm, and it changed from a nonmaterial and untestable phenomenon to a legitimate subject of scientific inquiry. Furthermore, because the NDE occurs in the mind, consciousness became a subject of scrutiny. If people were brain-dead at the time of an NDE, how could they have visions of any type, let alone ones of an afterlife? Did consciousness survive death?

The newly founded NDE field brought the spiritual world into focus at a time when materialism overshadowed the dominant culture.[24] Moreover, it introduced consciousness after death as a legitimate subject of scientific study. Thus, with the NDE, Moody shifted American societal awareness away from materialism toward spiritualism. He also moved societal attentiveness to consider consciousness after death as a possibility.

Thus, with the UFO phenomenon, humanity considered the possibility of life, and even intelligent life, "out there" in space. This information primed humanity to receive the knowledge that we were not alone in the universe. With the NDE phenomenon, people learned to accept the possibility of the afterlife, understanding that "death" was merely a journey in time, and that humans would exist beyond the grave.

Toward a New Paradigm

Religion provided humankind with a set of concepts explaining who had created them and the world (i.e., God), and where they went after they died (i.e., heaven or hell). The scientific method freed humanity from the bonds of religious dogmatism. Science created notions of *space* and *time* as mechanisms for understanding the structure of reality. People imagined that space and time existed "out there," independent of humanity and the Earth. For instance, a person might think, "The house across the street from me is 'there,' and it will be 'there' tomorrow when I go to work. It exists independently from me or anyone else seeing it."

Space and time, however, are mental constructs made by humans. They only exist because humans made them. Individuals held on to these notions so fervently because they existed for so long, and also because they have worked for so long. Humans take these ideas for granted, and, consequently, they take on a reality of their own. If people made them, they can *un*make them; or, minimally, *re*make them. This is exactly what is happening in the modern era. Humans are remaking *their* notions of space and time. They are freeing themselves from the bonds of a scientific method that envisioned space *and* time, and imagined things as *independent* of people. The scientific method served people well in understanding and measuring their world. Now this method binds people here.

Ideas are emerging from quantum physics (QP) that are akin to an era when science replaced religion as humanity's way of knowing the nature of things. At that time, people ardently believed in heaven; today, they believe just as strongly that space *and* time exist "out there," "independent" of humanity. There is a revolution of mind occurring, however, that is revealing only its outline. At this point, its meaning and direction are unknown.

In terms of quantum mechanics, random, endless, and floating probabilities of energy comprise the universe. It is as if the universe, and reality itself, consists of a gargantuan number of probabilities. Only when an observer looks at them do they take form (become particles). That observer then arranges these particles into patterns. From this perspective, conscious beings are creators of the universe.[25] The universe did *not* create humans.

Through a myriad of concepts, such as atoms, molecules, and the solar system, humans create the world (reality) in which they live. People make the world/reality understandable by means of concepts that create order and predictability. From this perspective, there is no physical world "out there" beyond people. There is only a mental world (within humans) that holds the concepts through which individuals look. As group members share these concepts with one another, they come to define what "really is." It is as if conscious human beings, after observing waves, then take particles (parts) and organize them to create a puzzle. The content of the puzzle (that is, its particular picture/image), can display anything.

For instance, at one time (776–146 BCE), the Greek mind presented humans with the concept of *reason,* which replaced a world controlled by gods. The Greeks employed the human mind in an effort to create a good and just person and society. When Isaac Newton arrived (AD 1643–1727), the puzzle's picture changed. A scientific approach replaced a world understood exclusively by an inquiring mind. A collection of facts to be tested replaced a mind seeking an understanding of perfect forms. People understood the world to be *independent* of observers, and *cause and effect* determined its shape of that world.

Today, QP is changing the puzzle's picture once again. No world exists "out there" *independent* of humans' conscious observation of it. Moreover, the world does *not* take shape by *cause and effect* acting upon it. Essentially, as long as there are conscious beings observing energy waves, the physical world exists. Yes, from this perspective *humans create the world* because their observation of it makes it real.

Why are we discussing QP in a book about the social worlds of aliens and beings in the afterlife? These phenomena are examples of "weird" manifestations in space and time, and they raise some challenging questions that are difficult to answer. For instance, how can aliens transport themselves over the vastness of space and time? How can they instantly appear to humans, and then just as quickly disappear? How is consciousness after death possible? Each of these questions lacks answers when one applies the scientific method to them. However, the questioner has a choice. If the scientific method cannot answer these questions, one must either abandon these questions as unanswerable or discover a different way of answering them. (Alternatively, if one truly believes in the scientific method, he or she could give up the questions as idiotic.) Ufologists and NDE researchers, of course, do not forsake these questions. For them, QP offers a promising framework for understanding the phenomena they study.[26] How so?

First, on the question of alien travel, QP has a concept, *nonlocality*, that provides a possible answer. Nonlocality describes instantaneous action at a distance.[27] Observation of an electron immediately affects its partner, regardless of how far away it is: A millimeter or twenty-five light-years! Ufologists may see nonlocality as a promising notion for explaining how aliens travel through the cosmos.

Second, as to aliens floating in and out of view, an explanation may be found in the QP notion of the *superposition state*, which describes "a physical thing [that] was in two places at the same time." To define the superposition state in another way, "Quantum mechanics says the method of looking creates the present situation of the atom concentrated in a single box or spread out over two."[28] Perhaps aliens arrive on Earth as waves of energy, but once observed by conscious humans, those aliens become visible to humans; conversely, when humans are not looking at them, the aliens disappear.

Third, in response to how consciousness is possible after death, we must again consider science. Classical scientific theory defines the brain as a physical entity, with the mind arising from it. "The implicit assumption made was [that] the relationship between brain activity and consciousness was always one of *cause to effect*, and never that of *effect to cause*."[29] Thus, when the brain died, the mind did too. The survival of consciousness after death of the brain/body was not possible in terms of this model of understanding.

QP notes, however, that the brain and mind are not the same. The brain is physical, while the mind is mental. There is a *dualism* in the physical world; that is, the mind and the brain are separate entities. The mind is not part of the brain. The mind is nonmaterial; the brain is material. In Chris Carter's book, *Science and the Near-Death Experience: How Consciousness Survives Death,* Rupert Sheldrake stated it this way: "If the conscious self is not identical with the function of the brain, but rather *interacts* with the brain through morphic fields, then it is possible that the conscious self could continue to be associated with these fields even after the death of the brain."[30]

As these examples demonstrate, UFO and NDE fields latched on to QP. This action served two purposes: (1) QP concepts are useful to ufologists and NDE researchers, helping to explain their "weird" phenomena, and (2) among the academic community, some question the legitimacy of ufologists and the NDE researchers, while others deny it. A latent function[31] of using concepts from physics, the preeminent field of science, is that it legitimizes the work of these researchers.

In sociological terms, we are witnessing a *social movement*[32] in its embryonic stage. This movement is creating a new reality (i.e., social construction of reality), and its change agents have names like Budd Hopkins and Raymond Moody. Jeremiah and Isaac were prophets when religion was the primary definer of reality.[33] Now, Hopkins and the others are arising as new prophets. They are leading humanity to consider that there is a plurality of worlds with intelligent beings on them. These creatures visit Earth and sometimes abduct humans. Therefore, the grays (good) and alien abductors (bad) are replacing the angels (good) and devils (bad) of yore.

These individuals and others are creating ideas and dispersing them through books, conferences, and organizations (e.g., International Association for Near-Death Studies [IANDS] and The Mutual UFO Network [MUFON]). The success of this social movement rests on its ability to secure resources, such as[34] organization (e.g., IANDS), mobilization (raising research funds), common goals and interests (e.g., articulated by NDE advocates), and opportunity (e.g., testimonials by UFO witnesses and NDE survivors).

This social movement is advancing the notion that *space, time,* and *reality* are mental products of an intelligent mind. It encourages people to understand these elements do not exist independent of the mind that created them. The human mind conceives space, time, and reality. The nature of these imaginations is being reimagined by the mind that imaged them.

Thus, the human mind is envisioning UFOs in space and explaining them as "other than" from Earth. As humans share this view with one another, it becomes real for them.[35] This process of visualizing is similar to the QP notion of waves becoming particles upon human observation. In a like manner, when a person experiences reality after his or her brain is dead, as in the NDE, this consciousness imagines a new place operating on uncertain principles. Consciousness exists beyond death, and, therefore, death is not the end. It becomes a transformation.

Medieval society persecuted Galileo and Copernicus because they went against the tide of religious belief. Today, people question Chardin,[36] Lanza,[37] Moody,[38] and others about the validity of their "outlandish" ideas. Again, these men are truly the social change agents of our modern time. They are opening the mind to new possibilities. One can only speculate where this will lead.

For instance, one can imagine that *nature* is a *mind*. It has quanta (i.e., units of energy) with myriad possibilities that materialized when a conscious mind observes it. It is as if millions of possibilities are holograms floating in the universe, and they materialized at the moment when intelligent beings (anywhere in the universe) view them. The phrase, "in the beginning," is the point when the process begins! On another level, when the process begins on a planet (e.g., Earth), there are millions of possibilities that are realized when thinking beings imagine them. For instance, when humans imagine these things, Earth's and humanity's place in creation materialize.

This mode of thinking moves people from a fixed understanding about the nature of things. Humans see that there are millions of possibilities that come into being only when realized. From this viewpoint, on one hand, reality becomes uncertain, scary, and relative. On the other hand, however, this viewpoint also leads us to acknowledge that reality allows all sorts of possibilities for humanity. Human wonderment and awe explode. Humans perceive the perennial cup as half-full or half-empty, only to realize that it is both. Humanity will move in the direction it puts its consciousness!

This book has come full circle. QP and the sociological approach, presented as the social construction of reality, assert a similar point. In QP, it is an observer's consciousness that results in a particular physical outcome (e.g., whether a photon is a wave or a particle). Essentially, QP asserts that the conscious observer *causes* physical reality. In sociology, as presented throughout this book, society *creates/constructs* reality. What QP states about physical reality is the same as what sociology states about social reality. As it turns out, humans are architects not only of the social world in which they live but also of the physical world that they inhabit.

APPENDIX A

HUMAN WITNESSES

Table A.1: Occupations of Human Witnesses

Education	Government/ Military	Professional/ Clergy	Science	Service	Skilled Worker	Unskilled Worker
Schoolteacher	Government employee	Architect	Astronomer (professional or amateur)	Baker	Aerospace worker	Cafeteria worker
Primary/ high school/ college/ graduate/ engineering student	Judge	Businessman	Geologist	Credit manager	Beekeeper	Cashier
High school/ college/ science teacher	Justice of peace	Doctor	Geophysicist	Locksmith	Bricklayer	Cow herder
	Mayor	Engineer	Physicist	Mail carrier	Fire tower observer	Farmer/ laborer/ farm worker

Education	Government/ Military	Professional/ Clergy	Science	Service	Skilled Worker	Unskilled Worker
	Active military/ veteran/pilot/ reservist/ airman/ soldier/ military officer/troop/ navy man	Explorer	Scientist	Nursing home worker	Jeweler	Fisherman
	Politician/US senator	Golf pro		Police officer	Mechanic	Grocery worker
		Lawyer		Ranch owner	Meteorological observer	Hospital worker
		Newspaper reporter/ journalist		Rock band/ musician	Oil driller	Hunter
		Nurse		Rubber plantation/ latex collector	Radar operator	Lineman
		Pastor/ minister/ seminarian		Security guard	Radio technician	Meat packer
		Photographer		Scoutmaster	Railroad manager/ station chief/ engineer/ conductor/ employee	Metal worker
		Pilot/crew/ airmen		Security guard	Stonemason	Miner
		Social worker		Surveyor	Technologist	Motorist

Education	Government/ Military	Professional/ Clergy	Science	Service	Skilled Worker	Unskilled Worker
				Telephone employee Truck/bus driver	Translator	Night watchman
				Traffic controller	UFO author/ investigator	Peasants
				Utility worker	Weather officer	Plant worker
				Waitress		Reindeer keeper
						Roofers
						Shepherd
						Trapper and guide
						Worker

APPENDIX B

TIME OF UFO SIGHTINGS

Table B.1: Number of Contacts per Year

YEAR	2011 Sample	+	2012 Sample without duplicates	=	TOTAL
1833	—	+	1	=	1
1860	1		1		2
1867	1		—		1
1870	—		1		1
1880	1		—		1
1889	1		1		2
1897	5		—		5
—Totals:	9		4		13
1909	1		4		5
1910	1		1		2
1917	—		1		1
1922	1		—		1
1927	1		1		2
1933	1		=		1
—Totals:	5		7		12

| | | 2012 Sample | | |
YEAR	2011 Sample	+	without duplicates	=	TOTAL
1940	—		1		1
1943	—		2		2
1944	1		—		1
1946	1		1		2
1947	14		14		28
1948	9		5		14
1949	7		5		12
—Totals:	32		28 (+1 for WWII)		60
1950	13		13		26
1951	2		7		8
1952	33		37		71
1953	14		10		24
1954	57		48		105
1955	9		14		24
1956	6		17		22
1957	15		13		28
1958	7		8		15
1959	16		11		27
—Totals:	172		178		350
1960	9		8		17
1961	2		3		5
1962	11		5		16
1963	8		8		16
1964	11		12		23
1965	27		22		49
1966	30		26		57
1967	51		41		92
1968	16		25		41
1969	25		29		54
—Totals:	190		179		370

| | | 2012 Sample | | |
YEAR	2011 Sample	+	*without* duplicates	= TOTAL
1970	13		12	27
1971	25		13	36
1972	7		12	19
1973	26		32	58
1974	24		23	47
1975	19		15	34
1976	15		20	35
1977	19		18	37
1978	29		26	55
1979	<u>17</u>		<u>17</u>	<u>34</u>
—Totals:	194		188	382
1980	9		10	19
1981	8		7	15
1982	12		4	16
1983	—		5	5
1984	4		5	9
1985	3		—	3
1986	6		7	13
1987	7		5	12
1988	5		13	18
1989	<u>17</u>		<u>12</u>	<u>29</u>
—Totals:	71		68	139
1990	17		6	23
1991	7		5	12
1992	15		6	21
1993	10		13	23
1994	14		14	28
1995	9		20	29
1996	12		17	29
1997	10		8	18

| | | 2012 Sample | | |
YEAR	2011 Sample	+	*without* duplicates	=	TOTAL
1998	6		9		15
1999	<u>12</u>		<u>8</u>		<u>20</u>
—Totals:	112		106		218
2000	12		15		27
2001	7		5		12
2002	3		4		7
2003	6		13		19
2004	6		12		18
2005	9		3		12
2006	3		3		6
2007	1		5		6
2008	1		2		3
2009	<u>2</u>		=		<u>2</u>
—Totals:	50		62		112
GRAND TOTAL:	835		821		1,656

2010, 2011, 2012 (Database has no cases past 2009).

APPENDIX C

WHERE UFOS WERE SEEN

Table C.1: Regions of the World with UFO Sightings

(2011 and 2012 Samples [*Excluding* Duplicates] Together)
[Countries in bold and italics indicate most
number of sightings in that region.]

REGIONS	COUNTRIES IN REGION			
			(2 samples combined; unduplicated)	
Africa—**23**	Algeria	1	Morocco	4
	Egypt	1	Senegal	1
	Ghana	1	*South Africa*	*10**
	Kenya	1	Zimbabwe/	3
			Rhodesia	
	Libya	1		
Asia—**64**	China	7	Lebanon	1
	India	3	Malaysia	9
	Indonesia	2	Mongolia	1
	Iran	2	Philippines	2
	Iraq	2	*Russia*	*17*
	Israel	2	Turkey	1
	Japan	8	Vietnam	2

REGIONS	COUNTRIES IN REGION			
	(2 samples combined; unduplicated)			
	Korea	3	Yemen	1
	Kuwait	1		
Europe—**478**	Austria	5	Italy	62
	Azerbaijan	1	Latvia	1
	Belgium	8	Netherlands/ Holland	2
	Bulgaria	1	Norway	1
	Croatia	1	Poland	5
	Cyprus	1	Portugal	7
	Denmark	11	Romania	9
	Estonia	1	Spain	42
	Finland	4	Sweden	16
	France	*181*	Switzerland	2
	Germany	13	Ukraine	3
	Hungary	2	United Kingdom (Great	95
	Iceland	1	Britain [England, Scotland,	
	Ireland	3	Wales] & Northern Ireland)	
North America—**944**	Canada	89	Panama	1
	Guatemala	1	Puerto Rico	11
	Mexico	12	*United States*	*830*
Oceania—**99**	*Australia/ (South Australia & Tasmania)*	*71* —	New Guinea New Zealand	3 25

REGIONS	COUNTRIES IN REGION			
	(2 samples combined; unduplicated)			

South	Argentina	49	Colombia	1
America—**156**	Bolivia	2	Paraguay	1
	Brazil	*63*	Peru	8
	Chile	16	Uruguay	2
			Venezuela	14

Table C.2: Countries with UFO Sightings

COUNTRIES	2011 Sample # of Contacts	2012 Sample (*Excluding* Duplicates) # of Contacts	Total
1. Algeria	1	—	1
2. Argentina	18	31	49
3. Australia/ So. Australia	27	44	71
4. Austria	—	5	5
5. Azerbaijan	1	—	1
6. Belgium	4	4	8
7. Bermuda	—	1	1
8. Bolivia	—	2	2
9. Brazil	35	28	63
10. Bulgaria	1	—	1
11. Canada	50	39	89
12. Canary Islands (Grand)	—	1	1
13. Chile	7	9	16
14. China	3	4	7
15. Colombia	—	1	1
16. Croatia	—	1	1
17. Cyprus	1	—	1

	2011 Sample	2012 Sample *(Excluding Duplicates)*	
COUNTRIES	# of Contacts	# of Contacts	Total
18. Denmark	5	6	11
19. Egypt	1	—	1
20. England/UK/ Great Britain	42	37	79
21. Estonia	—	1	1
22. Fiji Islands	—	2	2
23. Finland	4	—	4
24. France	84	97	181
25. Germany	4	9	13
26. Ghana	—	1	1
27. Greenland	—	1	1
28. Guam	1	—	1
29. Guatemala	1	—	1
30. Hungary	2	—	2
31. Iceland	1	—	1
32. India	1	2	3
33. Indonesia	1	1	2
34. Iran	2	—	2
35. Iraq	1	1	2
36. Ireland	2	1	3
37. Israel	1	1	2
38. Italy	34	28	62
39. Japan	5	3	8
40. Kenya	—	1	1
41. Korea	—	3	3
42. Kuwait	—	1	1
43. Latvia	1	—	1
44. Lebanon	—	1	1
45. Libya	1	—	1
46. Malaysia	4	5	9
47. Mexico	9	3	12
48. Mongolia	1	—	1

COUNTRIES	2011 Sample # of Contacts	2012 Sample *(Excluding* Duplicates) # of Contacts	Total
49. Morocco	3	1	4
50. Netherlands/ Holland	1	1	2
51. New Guinea	1	2	3
52. New Zealand	12	13	25
53. Norway	1	—	1
54. Panama	—	1	1
55. Paraguay	1	—	1
56. Peru	3	5	8
57. Philippines	2	—	2
58. Poland	2	3	5
59. Portugal	4	3	7
60. Puerto Rico	4	7	11
61. Romania	3	6	9
62. Russia/ USSR/ Soviet Union	10	7	17
63. Scotland	5	5	10
64. Senegal	—	1	1
65. South Africa	6	4	10
66. Spain	19	23	42
67. Sweden	9	7	16
68. Switzerland	—	2	2
69. Tasmania	—	1	1
70. Turkey	—	1	1
71. Ukraine	2	1	3
72. Uruguay	1	1	2
73. United States	393	437	830
74. Venezuela	9	5	14
75. Vietnam	1	1	2

COUNTRIES	2011 Sample # of Contacts	2012 Sample (*Excluding* Duplicates) # of Contacts	Total
76. Wales (listed separately from UK in databases)	4	2	6
77. Yemen	1	—	1
78. Zimbabwe/ (Rhodesia)	1	2	3
SUBTOTALS:	**854** +	**917** =	**1,771**
The following are *not* countries:			
Atlantic Ocean	1	5	6
Atlantic Ocean between Ireland & Iceland	1	—	1
Central Europe	—	1	1
China Sea	—	1	1
French-Belgium Border	—	1	1
Indian Ocean	1	1	2
Mediterranean Sea	—	2	2
North Sea (Over)	1	—	1
Pacific Ocean	—	1	1
Rugged Island	—	1	1
Sea of Japan	=	1	1
Total:	**858** +	**931** =	**1,789**

GRAND TOTAL: 1,789 (from 2 databases; unduplicated)
(*The following are* not *classified above: Antarctica-2, Azores-1, Bermuda-1, Borneo-1, Guam-1, Atlantic Ocean-6, Central Europe-1, China Sea-1, French/Belgium border-1, Indian Ocean-2, Mediterranean Sea-3, North Sea-2, Pacific Ocean-1, Sea of Japan-1, and Rugged Iisland-1* **Total = 25**)

Table C.3: US States with UFO Sightings

STATE	2011 Sample # of Sightings +	2012 Sample *(Excluding* Duplicates) # of Sightings =	Totals
Alabama	0 +	4 =	4
Alaska	8	4	12
Arizona	8	10	18
Arkansas	0	6	6
California	31	39	**70**
Colorado	11	12	23
Connecticut	8	7	15
Delaware	0	6	6
Florida	20	24	44
Georgia	4	7	11
Hawaii	0	2	2
Idaho	3	7	10
Illinois	20	13	33
Indiana	16	7	23
Iowa	7	5	12
Kansas	3	6	9
Kentucky	5	6	11
Louisiana	2	6	8
Maine	2	3	5
Maryland	3	5	8
Massachusetts	22	15	37
Michigan	14	15	29
Minnesota	8	4	12
Mississippi	—	3	3
Missouri	10	10	20
Montana	1	2	3
Nebraska	7	6	13
Nevada	5	6	11
New Hampshire	7	10	17
New Jersey	9	9	18

	2011 Sample	**2012 Sample** *(Excluding* Duplicates)	
	# of	# of	
STATE	Sightings +	Sightings =	Totals
New Mexico	7	8	15
New York	19	22	41
North Carolina	9	15	24
North Dakota	4	2	6
Ohio	19	36	55
Oklahoma	0	2	2
Oregon	8	2	10
Pennsylvania	16	17	33
Rhode Island	2	1	3
South Carolina	6	3	9
South Dakota	1	2	3
Tennessee	6	3	9
Texas	22	20	42
Utah	4	7	11
Vermont	0	1	**1**
Virginia	5	4	9
Washington	7	18	25
West Virginia	5	8	13
Wisconsin	9	3	12
Wyoming	1	1	2
(Washington, DC)	1	3	4
Totals:	**385**	**437**	**822**

NOTES

Preface

[1]   "*Xenology* is the scientific study of all extraterrestrial life, intelligence, and civilization." Robert A. Freitas, Jr., xenology home page, last modified January 6, 2009, http://www.xenology.info/.

Introduction

[1]   *Social science* is "a branch of science that deals with the institutions and functioning of human society and with the interpersonal relationships of individuals as member of society." Merriam-Webster Dictionary, https://www.google.com/#q=merriam+webster.

[2]   Some UFO writers claim aliens live in the center of the Earth. This book concentrates on societies found in outer space.

[3]   Sociology studies worlds created by humans, such as American and Chinese societies. The field utilizes concepts such as *institution, culture,* and *social class.* These terms are sufficiently broad to apply them to alien and afterlife societies.

[4]   David Liu and Ed Ksenych, "Content Analysis," in *Pleasures of Inquiry: Readings in Sociology* (Toronto: Thompson/Nelson, 2008), 442.

[5]   Ibid., 443.

Chapter 1

[1]   David Dressler, *Sociology: The Study of Human Interaction* (New York: Alfred A. Knopf, 1969), 3.

2 Gale Peter Largey and David Rodney Watson, "The Sociology of Odors," *American Journal of Sociology* 77, no. 6 (1972): 1021–34.

3 C. Wright Mills, *The Sociological Imagination* (New York: Oxford University Press, 1959).

4 Peter L. Berger, *Invitation to Sociology: A Humanistic Perspective* (New York: Doubleday Anchor Books, 1963).

5 Ibid., 29.

6 Initially, groups engage in a more or less conscious process of creating diagrams-for-social-living to solve problems-in-living. Members then use these diagrams over and over to solve their problems. At this point, they take the diagrams for granted, and they act automatically from them. The diagram-for-social-living has this configuration: ___|__|___.

7 The horizontal line in the diagram-for-social-living (i.e., ___|__|___) represents *all* possible human behavior. The two vertical lines distinguish appropriate group behaviors (i.e., inside the vertical lines) from inappropriate group behaviors (i.e., outside the vertical lines). For instance, in American society, having one wife is appropriate, whereas having two wives at the same time is inappropriate. Thus, the diagram has this configuration:
two wives | one wife | two wives. Diagram content changes. For example, in the United States, homosexuality was once outside the vertical lines, while today, in many places throughout the United States, it is inside these lines.

8 Two people constitute the smallest unit of study in sociology. The largest unit is society.

9 Food and shelter are examples of physical needs. Association with other humans is a social need. Humans are not born with the knowledge of acting in human ways. They acquire this knowledge from other humans.

10 Real needs are those humans must satisfy for their survival. For example, drinking water is necessary for humans' survival. People think perceived needs are necessary for survival, but they are not. For instance, many in the United States believe romantic love is compulsory for a relationship.

11 Adam and Eve experienced want after they fell from grace, according to Western Christian tradition.

12   Adam held a bush down, and Eve picked berries. Adam carried berries back to their shelter, and they both picked stems out before eating the berries.

13   Sociology identifies, seeks to understand, explains, and predicts the structure of human behavior.

14   Associated Press, "Peru Pushes Guinea Pigs as Food," CBS News, last modified February 11, 2009, http://www.cbsnews.com/2100–202_162–650148.html.

15   Deviant behaviors are outside the vertical lines on the diagram-for-social-living. Adam and Eve's diagram is:
Eat apples | Eat blueberries | Eat apples.

16   Power is the ability of person A to make person B do what B does not necessarily want.

17   People create diagrams in mostly nonconscious ways.

18   These ideas originate in a book by Johnson. The book is out of print.

19   This example demonstrates that everyone has diagrams-for-social-living. The content on these diagrams, however, changes from group/society to group/society. For instance,

Chinese Diagram: Eat hamburgers | Eat dogs | Eat hamburgers
American Diagram: Eat dogs | Eat hamburgers | Eat dogs

20   Michael Kimmel and Amy Aronson, *Sociology Now: The Essentials* (New York: Pearson, 2009), 44.

21   James M. Henslin, *Essentials of Sociology: A Down-to-Earth Approach* (Boston: Allyn & Bacon, 2011), 44.

22   This paragraph summarizes ideas from Johnson. The book is out of print.

23   This idea originated with Tischler. The book is out of print.

24   This paragraph summarizes ideas by Kornblum. The book is out of print.

25   This idea originated with Vander Zander. The book is out of print.

26   These cultures will remain primitive until they are westernized through globalization!

27   Raymond Scupin, *Cultural Anthropology: A Global Perspective* (New York: Pearson, 2012), 2.

28 Life is *social* when it happens in the presence of another person. This other can be as few as one or as many as a society.

29 NDE is an abbreviation for *near-death experience.*

30 Jim Pass, "What is Astrosociology?" Astrosociology Research Institute (ARI) home page, copyright 2008–13, http://www.astrosociology.org/.

31 Ibid.

Chapter 2

1 J. Allen Hynek is a former air force consultant to Project Blue Book. He founded the Center for UFO Studies (CUFOS).

2 *UFO* defined. Princeton University, http://www.wordnetweb. princeton.edu (broken link).

3 Dennis Stacy and Patrick Huyghe, *The Field Guide to UFOs: A Classification of Various Unidentified Aerial Phenomena Based on Eyewitness Accounts* (New York: Quill, 2000).

4 Charles Berlitz and William L. Moore, *The Roswell Incident: The Classical Study of UFO Contact* (New York: Berkley Books, 1980), 6–7.

5 This quote and information in this section come from: Dennis Stacy and Patrick Huyghe, *The Field Guide to UFOs* (New York: Quill, 2000), 2–5.

6 The Roswell incident home page: http://www.qsl.net/w5www/roswell. html.

7 Mass Media Distribution LLC, 2011: http://www.mmdnewswire.com/ roswell-1947-ufo-crash-finally-resolved-1727.html.

8 Project Blue Book Archive home page: http://www.bluebook archive. org. 1–5.

9 Ibid., 1.

10 Ibid.

11 Patrick Huyghe, *Swamp Gas Times: My Two Decades on the UFO Beat* (San Antonio, TX: Anomalist Books, 2001), 43.

12 UFO Evidence home page: http://www.ufoevidence.org/topics/ projectbluebook.htm.

13 Ibid.

[14] "Unidentified Flying Objects—Project BLUE BOOK." Freedom of Information Act (FOIA). The U.S. National Archives and Records Administration, http://www.archives.gov/foia/ufos.html.

[15] National security was the *sole* interest of the US military and government, according to many sources.

[16] Source is unknown.

[17] Material in this paragraph originates from an unknown source.

[18] Ufoinfo.com home page: http://www.ufoinfo.com.

[19] Wendelle C. Stevens's books may be purchased from UFO Photo Archives, Tucson, AZ 85710.

[20] A confidence level of 95 percent requires a sample size of 929 cases. A 99 percent confidence level requires 1,469 cases. The sample in the book exceeds both levels.

[21] *Demography* is the study of population. A demographic study identifies the social characteristics of a population, such as age, sex, and race. This book identifies the social characteristics of aliens and human witnesses.

[22] There are over 7,000 cases from throughout the world in Donald A. Johnson's On This Day databank. The databank's size prohibited analyzing all of the cases. Consequently, I analyzed two samples. Sample one held 835 cases, while sample two had 821. I drew the cases at different times (i.e., sample one in 2011 and sample two in 2012) to ensure consistency of results.

[23] A *median* is the midpoint in a range of numbers. Half the cases are above the median, and the other half of the cases are below it.

[24] A *mode* is the most frequently cited number. For example, 3 is the mode in this sequence of numbers: 1, 2, 3, 3, and 4.

[25] The tallest man ever recorded was Robert Wadlow of the United States. He was 8'11.1". The shortest man, Khagendra Thapa Magar, was from Nepal and stood at just 22". The average human is between five and six feet tall. "Average Human Height." Buzzle home page. http://www.buzzle.com/articles/average-human-height.html.

[26] Harold Garfinkel, an ethnomethodologist, studied how humans define sex. He found that they used ten rules. Significant among them was using the reproductive organs, thus identifying two sexes: males and females. Apparently, these rules are universal. Aliens identified only males and females among their species. Aliens seemed to use

reproductive organs as their criterion too. Harold Garfinkel, "Agnes," in *Tales from Wildwood: A Sociology for H.A.C.C.*, unpublished (Lexington, MA: Xerox College Publishing, 1973), 53–63.

27   People often use color to define different races. There is, however, only one race on Earth. It is the *human* race. Race is a notion created by humans, and it does not exist in nature.

28   The author's decision on this matter may be ethnocentric.

29   All quotes found in chapter 2 derive from cases in the On This Day databank. "On This Day," Ufoinfo.com, http://www.ufoinfo.com/onthisday/calendar.html.

30   The suit mentioned most often in sample one was the "diving suit."

31   There are several accounts of humans having sex with aliens. Sometimes aliens force themselves on humans, while at other times humans had consensual sex with aliens. John Mack, MD, *Abduction: Human Encounters with Aliens* (New York: Scribner's Sons, 1994).

32   The witness was Senator Stuart Symington of Missouri.

33   How many miles are in one light-year? There are 5,865,696,000,000 miles/year, or 5.9 trillion miles!

34   The first Earth Day was April 22, 1970.

35   Caution is necessary when interpreting survey results. First, different polling organizations, at different times, conducted these surveys. Second, the surveys do not record the social characteristics of respondents, such as their sex and age. At best, readers can obtain a snapshot of people's attitudes toward these phenomena.

Chapter 3

1   Mr. Steven's collection of other planets included Andromeda, Coma Berenices, Itibi Ra, Koldas, Maringa, Mirassol, Pleiades, Reticulum, and Venus.

2   Artur Berlet and Wendelle C. Stevens, *UFO Contact from Planet Acart: From Utopia to Reality* (Tucson, AZ: UFO Books, 1987), 10.

3   The math does not add up in two ways! First, the UFO voyaged for thirty hours and covered 62 million kilometers at four hundred and five hundred kilometers per second. Converting meters into miles: The alien craft traveled thirty hours at approximately 895 to 1,119

miles per hour (mph). The spaceship traveled 38.5 million miles. The calculations, however, yield: 895mph x 30 hours = 26,850 miles or 1,119mph x 30 hours = 33,570 miles. According to the book, Acart is 38.5 million miles from Earth. Thousands vs. millions of miles makes a huge difference! Also, in another section of the book (i.e., "Important Questions Answered") the author stated that it took thirty-six to thirty-eight hours to go 65 million kilometers. In two sections of the book, there are two sets of numbers citing the hours and distance from Acart to Earth.

4   Undocumented quotes cited in chapter 3 originate in the four books under review.

5   The book implied crime ended on Acart. Artur, however, described a disheveled man in a restaurant who was a criminal.

6   Artur was abducted in 1958. The general public did not know about solar tractors and cell phones at that time. When the book was published in 1987, many knew of these things.

7   The author identified three different dates for the event that happened in 1982: September x (unidentified day); Monday, November 29; and Tuesday, November 30. Also, the author cited two different times of the day for the event's occurrence: 2:00 a.m. and 4:00 a.m.

8   The author recorded two different jobs for Joao, doorman and porter.

9   Rodolfo R. Casellato, Joao Valerio da Silva, and Wendelle C. Stevens, chapter 1 in UFO *Abduction at Botucatu: A Preliminary Report* (Tucson, AZ: UFO Photo Archives, 1985).

10   Stefan thought their eyes were "thoughtful, peaceful, and they were studying him in a quizzical friendliness." Stefan Denaerde and Lt. Col. Wendelle C. Stevens (Ret.), *UFO . . . Contact from Planet Iarga: A Report of the Investigation* (Tucson, AZ: UFO Photo Archives, 1982), 27.

11   The author seemed to contradict himself. If males and females are equal, how can females be *dominant* because they raise children? Dominant suggests inequality.

12   The author reported that Iarga had 6,000 people/square kilometer. This seems like a lot of people, until one examines Earth's population centers. For example, if Iarga was on Earth, it would be ranked number 39 in density. It would be situated between Guadalajara, Mexico (5,900 people/square kilometer) and Osaka/Kobe/Kyoto, Japan (6,400 people/

square kilometer). City Mayors' Statistics, http://www.citymayors.com/
statistics/largest-cities-density-125.html.

[13] If Iargans made a car every twenty seconds, that would yield three cars
per minute, or 180 cars per hour, or 4,320 per day. If they made 4,320
cars per day, it would take twenty-five hours to make 4,500 cars. How
long is an Iargan day?

[14] The Prayer Foundation, http://www.prayerfoundation.org/nicene_creed.
htm.

[15] One should not be surprised by these cultural judgments. When the
Old and New Worlds met for the first time, Europeans and Native
Americans judged one another.

[16] Robert Lanza, MD, and Bob Berman, *Biocentrism: How Life and
Consciousness Are Keys to Understanding the True Nature of the Universe*
(Dallas, TX: Benbella Books, Inc., 2009).

[17] This book presents UFOs and NDEs together in chapters 5 and 6.

[18] *UMMOAA* was their preferred name. (See p. iv.)

[19] Encyclopedia Britannica, online, http://www.britannica.com.

[20] Wolf 424 is a binary star comprised of two red dwarf stars. It is located
14.2 light-years away from Earth, in constellation Virgo, between
Vindemiatrix and Auva. Its celestial coordinates are: Right Ascension
17:33:17; Declination: 09:01:3. WordIQ.com, http://www.wordiq.com/
definition/Wolf_424_Star_System.

[21] This means aliens, as well as earthlings.

[22] A footnote on page 208 in the book referenced the Cultural Revolution
in China in the mid- to late-1960s. At this time, millions of Chinese
occupied labor camps. This period paralleled the same time that
Ummites came to Earth, and the book made note of it!

[23] Duchamp's painting, following the Cubist tradition, is an abstract
drawing comprised of jagged lines that give the impression or feeling of
a man going down stairs. To the average viewer, it is a "bunch of lines"
thrown together.

[24] In the novel *A Canticle for Leibowitz* by Walter M. Miller Jr., a person in
the future picks up a piece of paper, and he surmises it is an important
relic. In fact, it is a grocery list that a man dropped in the distant past
after a nuclear holocaust.

Chapter 4

[1] Pim van Lommel, MD, *Consciousness Beyond Life: The Science of the Near-Death Experience* (New York: HarperOne, 2010), 7.

[2] Ibid., 8.

[3] Ibid.

[4] This idea was inspired by a student in my *Sociology of Other Worlds* course.

[5] Raymond A. Moody Jr., MD, *Life After Life: The Investigation of a Phenomenon—Survival of Bodily Death* (New York: HarperOne, 1975, 2001), 10–102.

[6] Near Death Experience Research Foundation, copyright 1999, NDERF, Experience Research Foundation, Jody A. Long, JD, and Jeffrey P. Long, MD, http://www.nderf.org.

[7] Percentages do not equal 100 percent because of rounding.

[8] NDErs is an abbreviation for *near-death experiencers.*

[9] *Other* includes people who did not report seeing a tunnel, light, or both. It also includes those who were uncertain of one or the other element. Surprisingly, there were 31 percent who were uncertain they went through a tunnel, or who did not report going through a tunnel but still saw a light.

[10] According to the CIA, men live just over sixty-four years of age, while women live to sixty-eight years. CIA World Factbook, 2009, https://www.cia.gov/libary/publications'the-world-factbook/geoxx.htmls/xx.html.

[11] All quotes found in chapter 4 originate in cases found in the After Death Communication Research Foundation (ADCRF) databank. ADCRF home page, Jody Long and Jeffrey Long, MD, copyright 1999, http://www.adcrf.org.

[12] NDErs explained the *life review* was a nonjudgmental activity. This was unlike what they learned about it in church. Also, more content was in adult life reviews than in those of children. This was likely because of the fact that adults have lived longer than children have, and so have more to cover in their life reviews.

[13] Four cases reported no data. The "No Report" category lists them.

[14] John J. Macionis, *Sociology* (Saddle River, NJ: Pearson, 2008), 586–587.

15   (Short title) *Consciousness Beyond Life*, 69.

16   Females accounted for 43 percent of the cases, while males represented 39 percent. Nineteen percent had generic first names (e.g., Kelly), initials, or were not familiar American/foreign names. This made it difficult to categorize them.

17   After Death Communication Research Foundation (ADCRF) home page. http://www.adcrf.org.

18   (Short title), *Life After Life,* 10–102.

19   Cases in the ADCRF were inaccurately numbered. Although there were 1,274 cases listed, cases 453 to 548 were missing. These 41 cases yielded a total of 1,233 cases in the ADCRF databank.

20   At a 90 percent confidence rate, the error level is 3.2 percent, while a 95 percent rate is 3.8 percent. (See http://www.custominsight.com/articles/random-sample-calculator.asp.) I imagined an exploratory examination of other worlds in this book. Although I attempted a random selection of cases, I do not claim these samples to be scientifically "pure." Additionally, discerning between *this* and *other* world descriptions was difficult. For instance, a witness "went into a bar, and the background was fuzzy white." It was unclear if the person was describing this world or the next one. The book contains only descriptions that clearly depicted the other world.

21   David Croteau and William Hoynes, *Experience Sociology* (New York: McGraw Hill, 2013), 319.

22   Ibid.

23   James M. Henslin, *Sociology: A Down-to-Earth Approach* (New York: Pearson, 2012), 66.

24   One of Raymond Moody's NDE elements is *ineffability,* or an indescribable nature. (Short title) *Life After Life,* 15.

25   In an extraordinary case account (ADCRF case 1034), an NDEr claimed her earliest memory was just *before* her birth. She claimed, "[I saw] suddenly an indescribable light and whirling around; indescribable harmonious melody, peace, oneness with [it] all."

26   *Values* are statements of preference, or what is deemed worthwhile by a group/society.

27 *Norms* are rules governing group members. Norms distinguish appropriate, right, and normal behavior from inappropriate, wrong, and abnormal behavior.

28 This is ADCRF case 1257.

29 There were 430 cases. I lost two cases in transcription.

30 Most of what I reported was direct quotes from OWBs. Human interpretation of what OWBs said was limited.

31 In a few cases, part was a *direct content* and part was a *dream* rendition. I counted these cases as direct *and* dream accounts.

32 Human interaction is the subject matter of sociology.

33 (Short title) *Consciousness Beyond Life*, 67. Dr. Lommel studied people eight years after their NDEs in order to determine if, with the passage of time, the NDE still impacted their lives.

34 The *Baltimore Sun*, http://articles.baltimoresun.com/1999–04–26/features/9904260270_1_near-death-eperience-life-after-life-heaven.

35 "More Than 9 in 10 Americans Continue to Believe in God," Gallup home page, June 3, 2011, http://www.gallup.com/poll/147887/americans-continue-believe-god.aspx.

36 The remaining references to God deal with the effects of the experience upon NDErs. Their inclination was a greater belief in God.

Chapter 5

1 Dave Wood, chairperson of the Association for the Scientific Study of Anomalous Phenomena (Assap), writes, "It is certainly a possibility that in ten years, it (UFOs) will be a dead subject . . . Assap's UFO cases have dropped 96 percent since 1988, while the number of other groups involved in UFO research has fallen from well over 100 in the 1990s to around 30 now. . . . The lack of compelling evidence beyond the pure anecdotal suggests that on balance of probabilities that nothing is out there." Jasper Copping, "UFO Enthusiasts Admit the Truth May Not Be Out There after All," *The Telegraph*, November 4, 2012, http://www.telegraph.co.uk/news/newstopics/howaboutthat/ufo/96534999/UFO-enthusiast.

2 Gallup Poll, 1947, in http://www.ufoevidence.org.

3   Karl Marx, Part I, *Critique of the Gotha Programme* (Moscow: Progress Publishers, 1970).

4   Cultural absolutists or universalists maintain cultures can be evaluated. Hence, they hold some cultures are superior to others.

Chapter 6

1   Brian Weiss, MD, in Alan Ross Hugenot, *The Death Experience: What It Is Like When You Die* (Indianapolis: Dog Ear Publishing, 2012), 59.

2   A *pareidolia* is a psychological phenomenon involving a vague and random stimulus perceived as significant. Defined in http://www.paradelle.wordpres.

3   *The Great Unknown—Some Views of the Afterlife*, http://library.thinkquest.org/16665/afterlife.frame.htm. (website discontinued).

4   (Short title) *Consciousness Beyond Death*, 9; Sam Parnia, MD, *Erasing Death: The Science That Is Rewriting the Boundaries between Life and Death* (New York: HarperOne, 2013).

5   Steven J. Dick, *Life on Other Worlds: The 20th Century Extraterrestrial Life Debate* (Cambridge: Cambridge University Press, 2001), 6.

6   John J. Macionis, *Society: The Basics* (Englewood Cliffs, NJ: Prentice Hall, 2011), 52–53.

7   (Short title) *Life on Other Worlds,* 9.

8   Ibid. This section is a summary of Dick's material.

9   For instance, Charles Darwin's *Origin of Species* presented the theory of evolution. Sociologist Herbert Spencer adopted Darwin's famous dictum, the survival of the fittest. He explained that only the fittest in society survive. In a like manner, Orson Welles included in his famous radio broadcast, *The War of the Worlds,* astronomers' notion of a biological universe where life is possible everywhere.

10 Peter Berger, *The Social Construction of Reality: A Treatise in the Sociology of Knowledge* (Garden City, NY: Doubleday & Co., 1967), 4.

11 Ferdinand Tonnies, *Community and Society (Gemeinschaft und Gesellschaft),* (New York: Harper & Row, 1963, orig. 1887).

12 According to the *Los Angeles Times*, the best-selling video game in 2012 was *Call of Duty: Black Ops II* (Activision, 2012). See http://articles.latimes.com/2012/dec/05/entertainment/la-et-ct-call-duty-ops-billion-20121205.

[13] "Ancient UFOs in Artwork, Renaissance Art," Tripod.com home page. http://litiumdreamer.tripod.com/ufoart.html.

[14] Dr. Kenneth Ring notes, "In short, whatever the existing or anticipated technology of the epoch makes it possible to conceive, that, in conjunction with the dominant worldview, appears to dictate the identity and purpose ascribed to UFOs." Kenneth Ring, PhD, *The Omega Project: Near-Death Experiences, UFO Encounters, and Mind at Large* (New York: William Morrow and Co., 1992), 209.

[15] Much of the material in this section originates with: Steven J. Dick, "From the Physical World to the Biological Universe: Democritus to Lowell" (chapter 1) in *Life on Other Worlds: The 20th Century Extraterrestrial Life Debate* (Cambridge: Cambridge University Press, 2001).

[16] Ibid., 8.

[17] Ibid.

[18] Ibid., 12.

[19] Ibid., 6.

[20] Gallup Poll, 1947, in http://www.ufoevidence.org.

[21] NBC Poll, 2012, at http://nbcnews.com/science/when-aliens-call-wholl-answer-850200.

[22] (Short title) *Life After Life*, x.

[23] Ibid., preface.

[24] Ibid., x.

[25] (Short title) *Biocentrism*.

[26] Although QP describes the behavior of atoms on the subatomic level, most physicists recognize this model applies to the macro level of the universe.

[27] Chris Carter, *Science and the Near-Death Experience: How Consciousness Survives Death* (Rochester, VT: Inner Traditions, 2010), 56–57.

[28] Bruce Rosenblum and Fred Kuttner, *Quantum Enigma: Physics Encounters Consciousness* (New York: Oxford University Press, 2006), 79.

[29] (Short title) *Science and the Near-Death Experience*, 13.

[30] Ibid., 98.

[31] A *latent function* is an unrecognized and unintended consequence of any social pattern. (Short title) *Society: The Basics*, 518.

32   A *social movement* is any organized activity that encourages or discourages social change. Edward Brent and J. Scott Lewis, *Sociology* (Burlington, MA: Jones & Bartlett Learning, 2014), 717.

33   Religion replaced paganism as a worldview. Now the UFO and NDE phenomena are replacing religion.

34   Anthony Giddens, Mitchell Duneier, Richard P. Appelbaum, and Deborah Carr, *Essentials of Sociology* (New York: W.W. Norton & Co., 2013), 519.

35   The Thomas Theorem states, "Situations defined as real are real in their consequences." (Short title) *Society: The Basics*, 99.

36   Pierre Teilhard de Chardin, *The Future of Man* (New York: Harper and Row, 1964).

37   (Short title) Robert Lanza, MD, with Bob Berman, *Biocentrism*.

38   (Short title) Raymond A. Moody, Jr., MD, *Life After Life*.

REFERENCES

Books

Alexander, Eben, MD. *Proof of Heaven: A Neurosurgeon's Journey into the Afterlife.* New York: Simon & Schuster Paperbacks, 2012.

Alexander, John B., PhD. *UFOs: Myths, Conspiracies, and Realities.* New York: St. Martin's Press, 2011.

Bailey, Lee W., and Jenny Yates. *The Near-Death Experience.* New York: Routledge, 1996.

Berger, Peter L. *Invitation to Sociology: A Humanistic Perspective.* New York: Doubleday Anchor Books, 1963.

Berger, Peter L., and Thomas Luckman. *The Social Construction of Reality: A Treatise in the Sociology of Knowledge.* Garden City, NY: Anchor Books, Doubleday & Co., Inc., 1966.

Berlet, Artur. *UFO Contact from Planet Acart: From Utopia to Reality.* Tucson, AZ: privately published by Wendelle C. Stevens, 1987.

Berlitz, Charles, and William L. Moore. *The Roswell Incident: The Classic Study of UFO Contact.* New York: Berkley Books, 1980.

Brent, Edward, and J. Scott Lewis. *Sociology.* Burlington, MA: Jones & Bartlett Learning, 2014.

Carter, Chris. *Science and the Near-Death Experience: How Consciousness Survives Death.* Rochester, VT: Inner Traditions, 2010.

Casellato, Rodolfo R., Joao Valerio da Silva, and Wendelle C. Stevens. *UFO Abduction at Botucatu: A Preliminary Report.* Tucson, AZ: privately published by Wendelle C. Stevens, 1985.

Croteau, David, and William Hoynes. *Experience Sociology.* New York: McGraw Hill, Co., 2013.

De Chardin, Pierre Teilhard. *The Future of Man.* New York: Harper & Row, 1964.

Denaerde, Stefan, with Amy Davidson, ed. *UFO … Contact from Planet Iarga.* Tucson, AZ: privately published by Wendelle C. Stevens, 1982.

Dick, Steven J. *Life on Other Worlds: The 20th Century Extraterrestrial Life Debate.* Cambridge: Cambridge University Press, 1998.

Dressler, David. *Sociology: The Study of Human Interaction.* New York: Alfred A. Knopf, 1969.

Eadie, Betty J. *Embraced by the Light.* Placeville, CA: Gold Leaf Press, 1992.

Fowler, Raymond. *The Andreasson Affair: The Documented Investigation of a Woman's Abduction Aboard a UFO.* Englewood Cliffs, NJ: Prentice Hall, Inc., 1979.

Friedman, Stanton T., MSc, and Kathleen Marden. *Captured! The Betty and Barney Hill UFO Experience.* Franklin Lakes, NJ: New Page Books, 2007.

Fuller, John G. *The Interrupted Journey.* New York: Dell, 1966.

Garfinkel, Harold. *Studies in Ethnomethodology.* Englewood Cliffs, NJ: Prentice-Hall, 1967.

Giddens, Anthony, Mitchell Duneier, Richard P. Appelbaum, and Deborah Carr. *Essentials of Sociology.* 4th ed. New York: W.W. Norton & Co., 2013.

Henslin, James M. *Sociology: A Down-to-Earth Approach.* 11th ed. New York: Pearson, 2012.

Hopkins, Budd. *Intruders: The Incredible Visitations at Copley Woods.* New York: Ballantine Books, 1987.

. *Missing Time.* New York: Ballantine Books, 1981.

Huyghe, Patrick. *Swamp Gas Times: My Two Decades on the UFO Beat.* San Antonio, TX: Anomalist Books, 2001.

. *The Field Guide to Extraterrestrials: A Complete Overview of Alien Lifeforms—Based on Actual Accounts and Sightings.* New York: Avon Books, 1996.

Jacobs, David M., ed. *UFOs & Abductions: Challenging the Borders of Knowledge.* Lawrence, KS: University Press of Kansas, 2000.

Jordan, Debbie, and Kathy Mitchell. *Abducted: The Story of Intruders Continues.* New York: Dell, 1994.

Kean, Leslie. *UFOs: Generals, Pilots, and Government Officials Go on the Record.* New York: Harmony Books, 2010.

Krapf, Phillip H. *The Contact Has Begun: The True Story of a Journalist's Encounter with Alien Beings.* Carlsbad, CA: Hay House, 1998.

. *The Challenge of Contact: A Mainstream Journalist's Report on Interplanetary Diplomacy.* Mount Shasta, CA: Origin Press, 2003.

Ksenych, Ed, and David Liu. *The Pleasure of Inquiry: Readings in Sociology*. Toronto: Thompson, 2008.

Lanza, Robert, MD, with Bob Berman. *Biocentrism: How Life and Consciousness Are the Keys to Understanding the True Nature of the Universe*. Dallas: Benbella Books, Inc., 2009.

Largey, Gale Peter, and David Rodney Watson. "The Sociology of Odors." *American Journal of Sociology* 77, no. 6, 1021–34.

Macionis, John J. *Society: The Basics*. 11th ed. New York: Pearson, 2011.

Mack, John E., MD. *Abduction: Human Encounters with Aliens*. New York: Charles Scribner's Sons, 1994.

. *Passport to the Cosmos: Human Transformation and Alien Encounters*. New York: Crown Publishers, 1999.

Marx, Karl. *Criticism of the Gotha Program*. Moscow: Progress Publ., 1970.

Miller, Walter M. *A Canticle for Leibowitz*. New York: HarperCollins, 1960.

Mills, C. Wright. *The Sociological Imagination*. New York: Oxford University Press, 1959.

Moody, Raymond A. Jr., MD. *Life After Life: The Investigation of a Phenomenon—Survival of Bodily Death*. New York: HarperOne, 1975, 2001.

. *Glimpses of Eternity: Sharing a Loved One's Passage from This Life to the Next*. New York: Guideposts, 2010.

———. *Reflection on Life After Life: More Discoveries in the Ongoing Investigation of Survival of Life After Bodily Death.* New York: Bantam Books, 1977.

Morse, Melvin, MD, with Paul Perry. *Closer to the Light: Learning from the Near-Death Experiences of Children.* New York: Ivy Books, 1990.

Parnia, Sam, MD. *Erasing Death: The Science That Is Rewriting the Boundaries between Life and Death.* New York: HarperOne, 2013.

Pearce, Joseph Chilton. *The Death of Religion and the Rebirth of Spirit: A Return to the Intelligence of the Heart.* Rochester, VT: Park Street Press, 2007.

Ribera, Antonio, with Cece Stevens, ed. *UFO Contact from Planet Ummo: The Incredible Truth,* Vol. II. Tucson, AZ: privately published by Wendelle C. Stevens, 1985.

Ring, Kenneth, PhD. *The Omega Project: Near-Death Experiences, UFO Encounters, and the Mind at Large.* New York: William Morrow & Co., 1992.

Ritchie, George G., with Elizabeth Sherrill. *Return from Tomorrow.* Grand Rapids, MI: Baker Book House, 1978.

Roberts, A. R. *From Adam to Omega: An Anatomy of UFO Phenomena.* Bloomington, IN: iUniverse, 2012.

Romanek, Stan, with J. Allan Danelek. *Messages: The World's Most Documented Extraterrestrial Contact Story.* Woodbury, MN: Llewellyn, 2009.

Rosenblum, Bruce, and Fred Kuttner. *Quantum Enigma: Physics Encounters Consciousness.* New York: Oxford University Press, 2006.

Scupin, Raymond. *Cultural Anthropology: A Global Perspective.* 8th ed. New York: Pearson, 2012.

Stacy, Dennis, and Patrick Huyghe. *The Field Guide to UFOs: A Classification of Various Unidentified Aerial Phenomena based on Eyewitness Accounts.* New York: HarperCollins, 2000.

Strieber, Whitley. *Communion: A True Story.* New York: Avon Books, 1987.

Tonnies, Ferdinand. *Community and Society (Gemeinschaft und Gesellschaft).* New York: Harper & Row, 1963.

Turok, Neil. *The Universe Within: From Quantum to Cosmos.* Toronto: House of Anansi Press, 2012.

Van Lommel, Pim, MD. *Consciousness Beyond Life: The Science of the Near-Death Experience.* New York: HarperOne, 2010.

Varghese, Roy Abraham. *There Is Life After Death: Compelling Reports From Those Who Have Glimpsed the After-Life.* Franklin Lakes, NJ: New Page Books, 2010.

Wolf, Fred Alan. *Parallel Universes: The Search for Other Worlds.* New York: Simon & Schuster, 1988.

Websites

http://www.adcrf.org (NDE data).

http://www.archieves.gov/foia/ufos.html (governmental archival information about UFOs).

http://www.astrosociology.org (definition of Astrosociology).

http://articles.baltimoresun.com/1999–04–26/features/9904260270_1_
near-death-experience-life-after-life-heaven (NDErs divorce rate).

http://www.bluebookarchieve.org (information on Project Blue Book).

http://www.britannica.com (characteristics of wolf star).

http://www.buzzle.com/articles/average-human-height.html
(information on human heights).

http://www.cbsnews.com/2100–202_162–650148.html (Peruvian
eating habits).

https://www.cia.gov/library/publications/the-world-factbook/
geoxx.htmls/xx.html (information on world-wide demographic
information).

http://www.citymayors.com/statistics/largest-cities-density-125.html
(information on city sizes).

http://www.custominsight.com/articles/random-sample-calculator
.asp (random numbers generator).

http://articles.latimes.com/2012/dec/05/entertainment/la-et-ct-call
-duty-ops-billion-20121205. (data on best-selling video games).

http://www.library.thinkquest.org/16665/afterlife.frame.htm (ancient
Egyptian afterlife practices).

http://www.litumdreamer.tripod.com/ufoart.html (ancient UFOs).

http://www.mmdnewswire.com/roswell-1947-ufo-crash-finally
-resolved-1727.html (information on the Roswell incident).

http://nbcnews.com/science/when-aliens-call-wholl-answer-850200
(information on public opinion on aliens visiting Earth).

http://www.nderf.org (NDE data).

http://www.paradelle.wordpres (definition of pareidolia).

http://www.prayerfoundation.org/nicene_creed.htm (Nicene Creed).

http://www.qsl.net/w5www/roswell.html (information on the
Roswell incident).

http://www.telegraph.co.uk/news/newstopics/howaboutthat
//ufo/9653499/UFO-enthusiast (explanation for diminished
UFO numbers).

http://www.ufoevidence.org (information on 1947 Gallup poll).

http://www.ufoevidence.org/topics/project bluebook.htm
(clarification of different governmental UFO projects).

http://www.ufoinfo.com ("On This Day" data on aliens and UFOs).

http://www.wordiq.com/definition?Wolf_424_Star_System
(definition of wolf star with dwarf star).

http://www.wordnetweb.princeton.edu (definition of *flying saucer*).

http://www.xenology.info (definition of *xenology*).